Return to Innocence

My Journey to Claim Wholeness

From Ancestral Ritual Abuse

Beth M. Bennett

Return to Innocence:
My Journey to Claim Wholeness from Ancestral Ritual Abuse

© 2020 by Beth M. Bennett
All rights reserved.

Photography: Faye and Patrick Bates
Front Cover Art: Oracle of the Crows, by Beth Bennett

Printed in the United States of America

First Printing: 2020

Paperback ISBN: 978-1-62747-337-8
eBook ISBN: 978-1-62747-339-2

Visit my Website at: bethmbennett.com

DEDICATION

I dedicate this book to the Souls of all who have ever walked this earth, desiring to be free from enslavement and wanting to return to their natural, loving, innocent state of being.

Table of Contents

Acknowledgements

There are many human angels who have supported my journey and shown me what Love truly is.

Thank you, Dawn, for the commitment we made pre-birth to do this journey as sisters. I love you more than words can express.

Thank you to my children who have provided much inspiration to remain on this healing path. I keep you always in my heart.

I acknowledge my inner children for enduring the journey so that my soul could finally remember Love. You are the amazing heroes of this journey.

Thank you to Robin Duda, Joseph Duda, and Ahara Vatter. You were my healing facilitators on the Sustainable Love Team. Your commitment to love, truth, and healing is extraordinary. Your capacity to shine your light so that the shadow might be seen, embraced, and healed has been your gift to me.

Robin, this book would not have been written without your deep commitment to my process, both as a practitioner in healing my wounds and as a writing coach for this book. Thank you for never giving up on me. Because you continued to hold me with love, I was able to return again and again to my own self-love. As I revisited my healing journey while I wrote this book, your loving spirit supported me to go deeper into my original material which allowed further integration for me. Your contribution to the clear articulation of my healing sessions was essential. I am grateful for your capacity to recall the energies that were present in the sessions so that the reader can truly receive the flavor of the energies being expressed. I am honored to know you as a being who is totally committed to your own healing process through expanding your Love. You are someone who walks your talk, and you continue to catalyze healing every day, through living in your authentic nature, willing to be truly yourself. Your commitment to seeing the birth of this book has been extraordinary.

Joseph, you have the distinction of being the first male that I ever trusted. I felt safe in your compassionate presence which allowed me to dive deeply into my soul's memories that were so full of shame. With your multidimensional architectural gifts, you constructed a safe space for our sessions, while helping me navigate the multidimensional portals to retrieve my fragmented soul and body. Your capacity to work with unity beings beyond the veil on my behalf allowed me to heal on the deepest level possible. I am so grateful for your willingness to lend your gifts to my healing journey. Because of you, I now know that I can be in friendship with men and feel safe.

Ahara, your nurturing heart was always with me through your words, your eyes, and your touch. Your presence as my Sacred Steward during Intensives allowed my body to feel safe once again and trust its own knowing. Your mastery and multidimensional understanding showed up through your hands. Not only did you nurture me through massage and through the nights of integration, your gifts in water as a Watsu practitioner allowed me to rebirth love with my sister. With your wise hands, you helped me ground the wisdom deeply into my body. Your commitment to my healing allowed me to journey into the depths of my shadow and go all the way through to the other side, always gazing into my soul with love and compassion, pointing the way to joy.

Faye, you have been my cheerleader extraordinaire, fulfilling so many roles in my life. From assisting me with the early writing process, to lending your support with Patrick for photography, to creating your divinely inspired bronze sculpture, *Courageous Heart*, which now graces my home, you have become someone whose friendship I treasure so deeply. Your enduring belief in me is felt each time I gaze at *Courageous Heart*, who radiates the essence of love and courage needed for my healing journey.

Many thanks to my fellow Sustainable Love friends. Our individual journeys of personal healing support us all.

To all the loving beings, those mentioned and many others too numerous to name, thank you from the bottom of my heart!

ORACLE OF THE CROWS

In June 2019, I began an intuitive painting class, *Paint Big, Live Big*, facilitated by Julie Claire. This class provided a playful venue for my self-expression, and the judgment-free zone that Julie insisted upon helped me to expand my acceptance of myself and my creations. As I was working on the last chapters of this book, the themes of my life were playing out in my painting process. I had been praying for support for my journey, and I specifically asked for help from beyond the veil in finishing my current painting and my book. At one point, a whoosh of energy quietly descended through the top of my head as I recognized that black crows had come into my painting and were there to support me. Eventually, I chose *Oracle of the Crows* to become my book cover.

I consulted the Medicine Cards (Sams and Carson, 1999) to further understand the messages from the crows. These words caught my eye: "All sacred texts are under the protection of Crow..." (p. 133). "Crow is an omen of change... Crow merges light and darkness, seeing both inner and outer reality" (p. 134).

There was one more message from Crow that I took into my heart. "With Crow medicine, you speak in a powerful voice when addressing issues that for you seem out of harmony, out of balance, out of whack, or unjust" (Sams and Carson, p. 134). From these words, I feel empowered by Crow to know and express the medicine of Truth as I speak out about the secrets of our world. I am grateful for Crow medicine and am humbled by Crow's blessing.

Prologue

Imagine awakening one day to discover that you had been living another life that you knew nothing about. The self that you had identified with for forty years was oblivious to other selves that were experiencing havoc and mayhem, violence and perpetration in times and places unremembered. Imagine discovering that the perpetrators of your life had tried to make sure that you would never ever remember any of it by erasing your memory because the induced amnesia covered up memories of the vilest crimes you could imagine. What would you do? What would you think? How would your life be impacted?

This book is the story of the unraveling of the amnesia and mysteries of my life. What is revealed has major implications for the life of everyone living on this planet. While this is my story, it is not as rare as you might wish. There are many others who live with ritual abuse and trauma which results in fragmentation, who continue in lives orchestrated by psychopathic controllers, most of whom are also victims and have no awareness of their own wounding and their own enslavement. This book may be the beginning of their personal awakening.

To uncover my story, I have had to be vigorously committed to the truth beyond my mind's reasoning so that I could listen to my soul and body's story. Finding my spiritual truth in my heart has been an amazing initiation into trusting the purpose of my life.

I had felt for a long time that I had a message to share with my fellow humans. Many years back when my first child was born, I could see myself, in my imagination, standing at a podium speaking to a large group. I knew there was something in my heart that I wanted to share with others, even though I had no recovered memories at that time. I carried an ongoing desire to inspire others to embrace life's challenges even while I had no conscious knowledge of the level of challenge that I had survived. I believed that there was purpose in everything that happened, that it was not just random bad luck when difficult, and even traumatic, events occurred. I believed there was rhyme and reason to our human lives that could be revealed if we humans were willing to look deeper into our souls and take responsibility for our lives.

When, at last, the memories began to surface, my beliefs were put to the test. Did I still believe there was purpose in experiencing the harshest of circumstances? Would I be able to open my heart and embrace the parts of myself that had been hidden? Could I find the rhyme and reason for my life?

From the time of the emergence of this vision of myself as an inspirational speaker, it would be more than a decade before I was aware that I had buried secrets from childhood that led to total amnesia as an adult, or some would say a split personality. During this time, I set about obtaining the two-point-five-children-and-white-picket-fence lifestyle. After leaving home and receiving my first college degree, I married a handsome man, held a respectable teaching job, and birthed two children. I had expected that experiencing these things would bring me a sense of fulfillment. But deep inside, most of the time, I felt alienated from others just as I had in my growing up years. I was starved for affection from a distant husband, and unaware of how I pushed him away. I felt helpless and easily angered when my children misbehaved. I did not understand why I could not relax and enjoy life more or feel close with anyone. I was constantly looking to the future for a time when everything would be "fine" and ignoring the persistent messages of my present that were telling me that I carried deep emotional pain with me every waking minute.

The pain of living a lonely, disconnected life and pretending everything was fine finally became greater than the pain of facing my truth. The recognition that I needed to investigate what these newly emerging emotions were connected to finally allowed me to receive helpful information. People and books came my way, and my personal awareness began to grow. Admitting there was something ominous dominating my life was a relief, even though I barely knew what that dark cloud was about.

It is a triumph to finally put voice to my experiences that were hidden for so long because exposing this information creates possibilities of healing not only for myself but for others. From the moment when I finally realized that I had experienced great trauma, I carried a deep desire for healing and wholeness. I had been saturated in the beliefs of the New Age philosophy, and I had always considered myself a spiritual person. With these beliefs, I created some lovely mental ideas about myself and my life. I did not have any idea what "wholeness" really meant for me, but it was a buzz word from the '80s that I had claimed for myself which described what I thought I needed. I knew, at least in theory, that I had the capacity to attract my heart's desires, even though I could not predict when, where or how.

In 2014, after many years of healing work and confronting what I am about to share, I made a commitment to bring meaning to my experience through writing this book, so that I could help others. I have been inspired when others have risen from the darkness of trauma and have received the gifts of love, becoming guiding lights for others. I desire to do the same.

What kept me moving forward was my inner knowing, my inner radar that created a resonance that showed me my next small step. Through my faith and strong desire to recover, I was eventually led to the perfect circumstances that introduced me to the presence of love and its power to heal.

First and foremost, I wrote this book for myself, to examine the many events that transpired during my childhood on into adulthood. Writing my story has demanded that I keep facing the truth of my life.

In this book I share my awakening from my ignorance, my strategies of denial, and my arrogance, into the truth of the universal process of healing trauma that takes us into our bodies and souls.

This is not an easy story to read, but I choose to share it because doing so is freeing for me, and there is the potential of opening the doors of awareness and healing for others. Dear Reader, I ask you to open your heart and your mind. There is a reason that this book is in your hands at this moment. This is an opportunity to know yourself more deeply by embracing your feelings and noticing your thoughts. As judgments arise, and they will, just breathe into them and let them be. You will need to trust your intuitive senses to truly receive this story, and I encourage you to pay close attention to your body sensations and feelings as you read. Your feelings are your connection with your own knowing, and that is how the soul communicates your spiritual wisdom and truth. This is the only real test you have of the veracity of *my* message and how it relates to you. Perhaps you have experiences in your own life that have remained hidden from your conscious self that you are ready to uncover. I urge you to seek support for your own healing when you are triggered by this information.

For those who are ready to know more of the truth of the forces that are spiritually manipulating us, I wish you the courage to embrace a grand awakening. What is not acknowledged cannot heal. In writing my story, I have digested it more thoroughly, and distilled my experiences into clarity and wisdom. The story itself is a sad, appalling story that becomes a treasure in my heart when the gems of wisdom reveal themselves. I hope you will discover some gems for yourself by taking this journey with me.

I have replaced the names of the participants with pseudonyms to protect privacy, except for the names of the three key individuals who are my healing facilitators, Robin, Joseph and Ahara. My sister, Dawn, has also consented to be identified in this book. I own each story shared as my very own and have no requirement that others remember things unfolding in the same way. Such is the nature of memory. Even individuals who share common, ordinary experiences, such as attending a birthday party, do not recall the events with the same perceptions and details. Traumatic events that have been repressed reach deeply into the subconscious, and their recall is totally unique to the individual. It is what has been perceived by the experiencer that creates the trauma imprint.

At this point in time, my purpose in sharing my story is to demonstrate that it is possible to heal these deep wounds. I have uncovered my experiences for the purpose of healing my family relationships, especially with my children and my sister, Dawn. My purpose is to live a loving life.

I am grateful to those who came before me who have courageously told their stories and who committed to healing their trauma. I am grateful to my sister, Dawn, who found memory of our familial abuse long before I did. I am grateful to Cathy O'Brien and other whistleblowers who have had the courage to tell the story of the unthinkable, unimaginable horrors of people abusing people.

My wish for you in reading about my journey is that you open to more self-love and self-discovery.

THIS BOOK CAN BE VERY TRIGGERING FOR SURVIVORS OF ABUSE. PLEASE EXERCISE EXTREME SELF CARE AND BE RESPONSIBLE FOR YOURSELF BY SEEKING THE SUPPORT THAT YOU NEED FOR ANY ISSUES THAT ARISE.

CHAPTER ONE

The Good Little Girl

HINTS FROM MY BABY BOOKS

As I have come out of denial throughout the years of uncovering abuse memories, what was done to me and what I passed down to my children, I brought new eyes to looking at the baby books of my birth. In 2017 I revisited these books, wondering what revealing information I might glean from the entries of my mother. I felt like a detective assigned to a very important case: Me.

I had concluded that my programming began at birth, and probably in my mother's womb, as is often the custom in families like mine. Indeed, as I read the entries of my mother, there were hints about my untoward beginnings in life.

My ancestors' names are written in one of the books. I read the names out loud identifying those who have come before me and whose genetics and DNA I have inherited, the very DNA which predisposes me with the ability to compartmentalize experiences in my brain. I am aware that I have now chosen to heal my ancestral patterns of the past and to create something more loving for the future. I am excited about epigenetics (see Glossary) research that suggests we are not limited by our DNA inheritance, but that our traits can be turned on or off by environmental factors. And I am encouraged by the idea that one's power to heal goes seven generations backward and seven generations forward through the lineage. Yes, my heart wants this to be so.

On the next page of my baby book is a copy of my birth certificate. I have two different birth certificates in my possession. On one certificate, in the box designated *name of birth father* is listed my biological father; on the second certificate, which was issued after I was adopted by my stepfather, the name of my stepfather is listed as my birth father. At the time of adoption, my original birth certificate was sealed. Years later, new laws released this certificate to my mother, and she passed it on to me. As I look at the two certificates, I am incensed to think that the facts of my life could be changed with the issuance of a new birth certificate. *How dare them think that they can manipulate the truth of my birth!*

Flipping further through the book, I come to the page with instructions saying that I am to have three ounces of formula every four hours. My heart feels heavy. *I am sure I did not always want to wait four hours between feedings!*

Then comes the page that has an error on it. I was born on December 11, 1950. There is a picture of me dated December 25 saying I am one week old. I do the math. *No, I am two weeks old. Where is this confusion coming from?* A couple pages later is another entry by my mother, reiterating that I am one week old on Christmas Day. "*Made first outing on Christmas Day. Went to [City] Sanctuary to the Christmas Class. Heard Jesus' Dictation. Attended first class at exactly one week.*" My body shivers as I read this. I then remember an experience I retrieved during a healing session in 2017. My baby body is responding to cold metal; something mechanical is my comfort. There is no skin to skin warmth with my mother. Perhaps that is where I was in the missing week. I know now that they mind-swiped my mother. This horrendous fact hits me at the core of my being. *How could anyone be so heartless? Bastards!*

The entry on the next page of my baby book reads: "*Wanted to give up 10 pm feeding last four weeks instead of skipping 2 am. At six weeks forced to eat at 10 pm and cried it out at 2 am.*" Many years ago, my mother had told me about my father insisting that I be put downstairs to "cry it out" when I had awakened in the middle of the night, hungry and howling. In the morning when she went down to get me, my fontanel was sunken in.

I now know that denying human baby needs is protocol for cult programming. Deep in my baby soul I quickly came to know that crying would not bring what I needed. There were rules and procedures to be followed. I had begun my journey here on planet Earth. A deep sadness weighs in my heart. Sometimes I cannot bear to think of these abuses. *What kind of a planet am I living on anyway?*

MY PARENTS

All families have "facts" they report, stories they share. The following is what I have been told.

My grandmother on my mother's side had married a man who came with a strong gambling addiction. In the summer, using railroad passes supplied by my grandfather's office job in the Southern Pacific Railroad, my grandmother took my mother and my aunt to every "I AM" Activity gathering across the country, sometimes seven days on the train eating carefully thought-out meals from her basket. They ended up attending large day and night meetings in the Los Angeles

Shrine Auditorium. Due to my grandfather's gambling addiction, my grandmother was deeply disappointed in her marriage and this was her escape. My aunt rebelled against the cult rules. My mother adored the promises the cult made of purity and ascension. She wanted to remain in the cult. Now, I see how as a child, I took on my mother's attitudes and her kind of spirituality. She decreed daily (stating affirmations over and over) and desired to go into the spiritual realms and commune with Ascended Masters. She often wrote poetry expressing her spiritual understandings. A large picture of St. Germain hovered at the end of our hallway. As an adult, I have learned that there are entities who falsely present themselves as Ascended Masters to dupe individuals into giving their power to a false identity. I was connected to this false being and believe that my mother was also, while the authentic St. Germain eluded us. I admired my mother's spiritual life and wanted to emulate that too. I see now that this was the mental/spiritual manipulation that kept me in denial of my trauma and what was really happening to my body.

Mom told me that she met my father in the cult when they were teenagers. Around age twenty, he was drafted for World War II and sent to Germany, returning home in 1945. That summer they reconnected and attended a Youth Conclave Cruise sponsored by the cult. At eighteen, my mother was anxious to get out from under her mother's thumb and was grateful to be allowed to go on the cruise. In the fall a year later, they eloped. My mother sent a telegram to let her mother know she had married. I feel a wave of sadness come over me as I realize how the coldness and cruelty from her mother was passed down to me.

Going to Georgia Tech on the G.I. bill, my father earned his degree in electrical engineering, and they moved to the Southwest. He gained employment on a military base. As newlyweds, my father was in charge. He had to teach my mother how to cook and drive. As if she was a child, she followed him to the cult classes which she loved. Now I see the vulnerable young girl my mother was, so easily manipulated.

My sister, Dawn, arrived two years before me not long after my parents' arrival in the new town. I came along two years later. Mom told me, "I didn't know I was pregnant with you until four months after conception. You announced yourself with a few hard kicks against my stomach." *How could she be so numb as to not know she was pregnant?* After all, her pregnancy was evidence that she "did it", going against daytime messages about sex being shameful and wrong. The "game" was to deny sexual activity until the rituals of the night came alive.

NOT LIKE EVERYBODY ELSE

We were not allowed to eat meat or wear red and black or have pets, according to the rules of the cult. My father painted our red wagon yellow, and that seemed normal to me. My mother had a pink bedroom and my father had a deep purple one, separate from my mother. No dogs or cats were allowed in our house because they were believed to be evil human creations. "Get out of here. Go home," my mother hissed to any critters that wandered into our yard. To keep the dogs out of our garbage, she put chili powder in the trash cans. "See how you like that!" she threatened. I was afraid of animals. I expected them to attack me. The thought of having a pet to love never crossed my mind. I know now that we were not allowed to bond with animals so that we would be fully alienated from loving them, preparing us for animal cruelty during rituals.

I had playmates in the neighborhood and vaguely knew that they had different house rules. One time a friend's mother offered me a bite of pot roast that she was preparing. My curiosity won out and I popped it in my mouth, chewing a very tough lump of brown sawdust-like meat. I finally spit it out and hid the brown lump in my friend's toy box. I felt terribly guilty and worried that my family might find out about this violation of the rules. *But,* I rationalized, *I do not like it, so it does not count.* At eight, I accidentally discovered a can of meat in my mother's dresser drawer. *How on earth could Mom have that in her drawer? She would not eat meat. I know she could never do such a thing!* My head spun with this deception. I was so confused. This was typical of the double bind created by what we practiced during the day versus what took place at night.

I recall at six, standing on the sidewalk looking at whiny, red-hair Frances, and proclaiming like my father, "You have to love everybody, but you don't have to like everyone."

"No, you have to *like* everyone, but you don't have to *love* everyone," she argued.

"Well, there's a cataclysm coming soon," I announced, hoping to impress her with my superior knowledge.

"Uh uh," she muttered, vigorously shaking her head from side to side.

"You just wait and see," I said righteously with hands on my hips. "We are special. We are going to make our ascension, and you aren't."

SISTERS HOME ALONE

On Wednesday nights, my parents who are group leaders for the "I AM" Activity, leave Dawn and me, ages six and four, alone at home so they can lead an "I AM" Activity class. "Okay, girls. Stay in the house and go to bed at 7:30," my father instructs.

My knees start shaking as my parents go out the door. *What if someone comes to the house and rings the doorbell? Should we answer the door? What if it is a bad man who can hurt us?*

Who will put us to bed? A shiver runs through my body. I do not feel safe with my sister.

Dawn's defiance shines in her eyes as she peers out the window watching our parents drive away in the blue Hudson. I look at her for a cue to see what is next for the evening. With a glare of dismissal of the rules and me, she says, "If you want, Beth, you can go outside and play."

I run out the door and head up the street, knocking loudly on my friend's door. I am welcomed in but feel too antsy to relax and have fun. As the sun goes down, I escape her house, run the two blocks home, and dive in under my bed covers. I cannot get to sleep soon enough. I see now that my only escape from my terror was to go to sleep, a pattern that has stayed with me my whole life.

This was a daytime memory of feeling alone, unprotected, unsafe, with no guardian other than my six-year-old sister. I see now how disassociated and oblivious to the needs and feelings of children my parents were. Why else would they be so unkind? In the '50s, few parents were aware of their own emotional needs, much less those of their children. My compassion for my terrorized little girl has grown in my healing work, as I acknowledge those feelings of abandonment. Understanding that denial of needs was standard practice at that time does not erase the painful experiences that are etched deeply in my soul.

NIGHTTIME HORRORS

This is a memory that I retrieved in 2010. The mind and voice of my five-year old speaks.

Mommy and Daddy are in the car and my sister too. It is dark outside as we drive. My head feels funny.

Where did Mommy go? Where did Daddy go? I hear an animal squealing in pain. I am shaking. I look for Dawn. Who are all these people? Why am I here? I want to run away and hide. The squealing stops. I shudder. Am I next? This cannot be happening. Who is next? Is it me or my sister? They tell me I get to choose. No, no, no. Mommy, help! Somebody! Help me! Where is Dawn? They are going to hurt me. I am so scared. I feel warm pee moving down my leg. What are all these horrible smells? I cannot breathe. I am dizzy. I am going to throw up.

Frozen, I stare at the drippy, stinky goo. That is not me. That is not mine. I am leaving my body.

"*You are going to clean that up,*" *a stern voice bellows. I gag.*

"*Okay, I'll do it. Take me,*" *I say. "Don't take Dawn."*

"*Too late. We want your sister today,*" *the sinister voice commands. "Besides, you have a mess to clean up. We'll save you for next time."*

It should be me. If only I had not thrown-up they would not have taken Dawn. It is all my fault that they took Dawn.

I feel a damp cloth covering my face. There is that smell. I cannot breathe. I am floating away into no feeling, no body. I go unconscious.

As I am rising, I say to myself, "They didn't want me, but I'm safe for now."

A soft warmth surrounds me. "We are with you," soft voices whisper. I want to stay with them. I have been seduced into the other world. My little girl wanted anything but the torture.

"*But I must go back and find my sister. I love my sister.*"

I go unconscious.

I next thing I remembered was in the morning. I awoke in my bed, hungry, with no thoughts of the nighttime events. *Peanut butter. I know how to get peanut butter.* I quietly opened my bedroom door into the kitchen and padded to the cabinet where the peanut butter lived and tucked it under my arm, knife in hand, ready to relay that yummy taste into my mouth. I returned to my bedroom for the feast. It was smooth, soothing, reliable. Soon I heard my mother coming into the kitchen to make breakfast. I hid the jar of peanut butter under my bed. I guiltily opened the door into the kitchen again.

"Good morning, Bethie Doodle." My mother's voice is flat and high-pitched.

"Morning, Mommy." I worried that she would smell the peanut butter on my breath, but she just directed her gaze at the carton of eggs and plugged in the toaster. My father and sister joined us in the kitchen.

"Would you like jelly and butter on your toast this morning, or just butter?" My mother patiently looked my way.

"Uh, jelly and butter, no, just butter, wait, wait, wait, jelly and butter."

I carried intense anxiety over simple decisions, filling me with terror when making any choice. After retrieving memories about the double bind "choices" that I experienced in the night life, I now understood the consequences my trainers had emblazoned into my psyche. They always made me feel it was my fault when my sister got hurt, making any choice a double bind. This heightened my anxiety around simple choices throughout my whole life.

The complete denial of the terrifying events of the night before, which was typical of cult programming practices, cemented the split between my day life and night life. Indeed, there was a split in my mother, father, sister and then the soon-to-be-born twins.

THE TWINS ARRIVE AND I START FIRST GRADE

In the summer of 1956 right before I started first grade, my youngest siblings were born, a boy and a girl. I felt joy and excitement with this big family event. I wanted something, anything that would make me feel special. I craved positive, normal attention from others and was proud to show off "my babies" to my playmates. "They're *twins*," I gushed, "and their 'bilical cord will come off all by itself in a couple days!" I was proud that they were in *my* family. No one else in the neighborhood had twins. This normal, happy event felt like an anomaly in my life.

No longer the baby of the family, I tried to be highly obedient. *I have got to be a good big sister. Maybe I can be even better than Dawn. Oh no, one of the babies is crying. Somebody is going to get in trouble.* I rushed to their side. I jiggled the bassinets. Soon both babies joined in, and then *I* felt like crying too. Normal, human emotions felt dangerous to me.

In the fall, I was old enough for school. During the summer, my mother had begun to prepare me for this next big step in my life. "It's time to give up your naps," she announced. I loved my naps, but now I was a big girl. Then she added, "And you are going to have to make your bed every day before you go to school."

I began to fret. This new responsibility weighed heavily on my mind. Would I be able to do this? Deep down I feared punishment, unaware of the nighttime terror that always lurked within me. What if I failed? I did not dare forget! That simply was not a possibility. The night before the first day of school, I slept restlessly and in the middle of the night, awoke. I got out of bed and pulled the covers carefully into place, arranging the sheet, blankets, and bedspread with as much precision as I could muster. I then climbed back onto my made bed and drifted to sleep on top of the covers. I could relax, at last. A threat buried so deep motivated my actions. I had to be perfect or be punished.

The next morning, I trotted out the door next to Dawn, my chaperone in the evil outside world, whose duty was to get me to school. She had been negotiating the complex public bus system by herself to St. Vincent's Academy for the past two years. My father had chosen a Catholic school over public school, the lesser of two evils.

Will Dawn be able to get me to school safely? Will I get lost? My favorite part of the bus ride was the drugstore where we got off one bus and waited to transfer to the next one. I was infatuated with the candy section near the front door which remained open during good weather. Pungent cigar box smells, dusty containers, and the smelly exhaust from public transportation drifted to my nostrils. *Maybe one very special day Mommy will give me money for a candy bar. Payday. Yum, yum, yum. Reese's Peanut Butter Cups. Neccos. Wax juice bottles. Will I get on the right bus? What will I do if I miss the bus? Will Dawn remember to tell me to get on?* I yearned for a smile from Dawn, but she only tossed scowls of disgust and disdain my way.

Little about the Catholic school felt welcoming except Cecilia, my bit of warmth there. Against the cold, enemy environment of the *Outer World*, Cecilia and I became friends. She was cute, and I loved her curly brown hair. I giggled as I thought about how she smelled like mayonnaise. I did not always know what to say to other children but with Cecilia it did not matter.

On certain Fridays, everybody but my sister and me went to Communion. The playground was deserted, as our classmates scurried to chapel. We continued to play outside. I shivered in my boots, dreading the moment a nun might catch sight of us. Sure enough, on a cold, cloudy Friday, one of the Sisters appeared out of nowhere. Dawn and I were passing time on the swings.

"Why are you children outside?" she barked as my stomach lurched into my throat.

Dawn answered for both of us in her strong voice. "We don't have to go. Our father said so. We're not Catholics."

The nun hurried on. *What does that nun think of me now? How can I follow Daddy's rules and the school's rules too?* A jittery buzz ran up my spine. I expected punishment at any moment.

TEARS NOT ALLOWED

The one thing that I could be proud of was my learning at school. I was reading and jumping Double Dutch at recess and usually getting 100% on my spelling tests. *I am smart. I know how to do things. I think I will ask Daddy if I can try cooking dinner. Dawn can help too.*

"Daddy, can we make dinner tonight?" It was not long after the twins had arrived, and Dawn and I wanted to surprise our mother. We enthusiastically pulled chairs over to the stove, so we could reach the top. *I think Mommy will really like our dinner!* I was hoping she would praise me.

"Let's do enchiladas," Dawn announced. I did not argue because I liked enchiladas a lot, and we had Daddy's approval.

The table was set and the production line ready to roll: *Take a corn tortilla and dip it in the hot oil in the frying pan.* That was Dawn's part.

"Be careful, be careful, be careful," my father chanted every few moments. He was assisting Dawn as she dipped the tortillas in the hot oil.

Add a small mound of cheese in the center and roll it up. That was my part with my little five-year old fingers navigating the burning hot oil! I had kneeled on the chair to find the perfect spot to reach the counter next to the stove. Next came the red enchilada sauce, added by my father, with lavish amounts smothering the enchiladas.

At last the plates were served with great anticipation and pride.

My mother looked, paused with a blank face, and then took a bite of our enchiladas. "Oh, these are so tough." My mother scoffed as she tried to cut her first bite. "You left the tortillas in the oven for too long, and they got hard."

Tears began to roll down my cheeks. My heart had been pierced. Our lovely effort received no praise, hugs, or reward. The rest of my family was silent. In that moment, chewing became our only conversation. In my day life, I immediately shut down any efforts of normal kid curiosity. I had to be perfect. There was no room for taking a risk, exploration, learning new things or asking questions.

Upon reflection I see that I, as a child, cried the tears for the family, the tears that nobody wanted to feel or see. I constantly tried to suppress my tears. Dawn often teased me and called me "cry baby." By the age of six, I thought I was strong enough to stand up to her.

"If I hit you, you'll cry," she said one day.

"No, I won't," I declared.

"Yes, you will," she gibed.

"No, I won't."

"Yes, you will."

Whack! A sting on my cheek popped the bubble of my tears. I had been so sure I could endure the slap without crying. I felt angry, hurt, and helpless because I did not think I could make it in my world without her help, and yet she made me feel so bad.

My anger at Dawn buried itself deep inside, and one day it finally took flight. I was in second grade, and we were on our way home from school, tucked in near the back of the city bus on our brown upholstered seats, sporting our navy-blue uniforms (exempted from black by the Sisters).

"Where is my spelling book?" I asked. "Where is my spelling book?" I repeated, my voice rising. "Now I can't study," I squealed. "I won't be able to get 100%." Heat began to move through my chest and arms as panic and terror filled me.

Dawn suddenly pulled out my spelling book. It seemed to appear out of nowhere. My panic turned to rage. "You hid my spelling book on purpose!" I screamed, lifting my metal lunchbox high above her head and slamming it down without mercy. I felt satisfied seeing the grimace of pain on her face. My suppressed tears had become revenge. A big, red lump immediately rose on her head. It had happened so fast.

When we got home, my mother did not say much. My reputation as the good one went untarnished. *It was Dawn's fault because her bad trick started it all. Mommy still thinks I am a good girl.*

The programming that took place during the night rituals was designed to break the bonds between siblings. We were given impossible "choices" making us feel that we were the reason our siblings got hurt. While the conscious memories of the nightlife of these events were split off, the hatred and anger would leak out into our daytime relating. My torrent of rage at Dawn from times she had been forced to hurt me finally had found its expression on the city bus.

A LIAR AND A THIEF

In a strict, rigid, rule-driven home, the continual denial of sugar felt cruel. It was one more denial of love. One summer day, when I was seven years old, my best friend asked me if I wanted to go to the *7-11* convenience store around the corner to buy candy. I wanted to go. In fact, I *had* to go. *I never get to have candy, but I WANT SOME! I am going to beg Mommy to let me go.* I slipped inside my house to discover that she was in the shower. *Perfect! I will just get a dime from her wallet.*

Cinnamon red hots. They called to me from the display shelf. My guilt melted as I merged with the blissful taste of the sugary cinnamon beads on my tongue.

I returned home and boldly displayed the box of partially eaten red hots. "Kathy bought me some red hots, Mommy," I stated as a matter of fact.

"Oh, how nice of her." My mother's own sweet tooth kicked in. "Let me have a few," she pleaded. I readily complied, eagerly distracting her from the rest of my deception of stealing her money.

That same summer, lying and deceiving continued in me and my sister. Dawn was stealing bottled cokes from the corner filling station and sometimes taking me along. I could not believe how I lucked out the day she got caught because I was not with her. The uniformed filling station attendant marched her down the street several blocks to our house to report to my mother what she had done. *I am a good girl. Dawn is the one getting in trouble.* My body quivered as the tense story unfolded in her bedroom when my father got home. In the day life, my father never spanked or hit us. The punishment was crueler than that. Sometimes he would refuse to speak to or look at Dawn for several days at a time, as if she were dead to him. I hoped to never be invisible to my father, so I decided early on to go to the opposite polarity and always do and be exactly what was expected. *I will be a better girl than Dawn and do whatever it takes to not be erased.*

"I don't know what we are going to do about Dawn," I overheard my father say to my mother.

"I'll say some decrees to St. Germain," my mother offered. "At least Beth isn't like that." The sound of her sigh reached deep into my heart. *I am her good girl. I am her good girl.* It felt like my very life depended on believing just that!

My compliance and eagerness to be good and please my father was firm. And my need for his approval eclipsed my humiliation and shame, anxious for his love and attention.

"Beth, it's time for your enema." My father is calling me into the bathroom. I have a sore throat and fever. *I hate enemas. They make my belly hurt. I wish Mommy could do it.* My sphincter muscles pull in, my arms cross tightly over my chest, my hands become fists as my breath shortens. I dare not speak my "no".

The cloth bathmat is ready for me. I fold over face down on my knees with only my pajama top on, knowing that he will soon be poking that white thing into my bottom where the poop comes out. *I wish I could run away and hide. But I want Daddy to be proud of me. I will not make a fuss.* My small self is determined to endure.

The water from the rubber bag begins to flow. It feels cold. "Tell me when you feel full but try to hold it as long as you can," my father instructs.

My belly is about to burst. "Ok," I say. He shuts down the clamp to the water flow, and I rush to the toilet. *Why can't Mommy do this? Why is Daddy the one who gives the enemas?*

"Just a couple more times," my father says with a smile, and I obediently assume the humiliating position on the floor, carefully studying the pink and green flowers in the bathroom rug. I fixate on the flower patterns; I feel nothing.

I am finally done. I look at my father's face. It looks strange to me with an eerie twist of his mouth and a vacant stare. I receive his implied message that says, "Good girls like enemas when they are sick. I give you enemas because I love you."

A POLARIZED, SPLIT LIFE

In counseling sessions after retrieving many childhood memories, I began to understand that I had absorbed my mother's feelings entirely. As I grew, I attempted to find a sense of safety by making sure my mother was happy, and by developing a blind allegiance to my father's rigid rules and expectations. Not upsetting my mother or father through obedience to the rules was the guiding force of my life. This hypervigilant monitoring made me a very anxious, worried child. It was an illusion that I had any control over my life at all. We were in the hands of the cult.

I knew my family as members of a wonderful love and light group, where we shunned the evil of the world. Daytime meant Ascended Masters, pastel colors, being harmonious and pure, no meat, no sex, no animals. As an adult, I felt disdain and mistrust of "love and light" because of the satanic programming that intentionally wanted to separate me from my body's natural loving impulses, a split between spirit and form. This spiritual programming inverted the true loving essence of God/Source. The black of night meant worshipping Satan, rage, terror, torture, depraved sex, the red blood of killing and cannibalism.

To most people, we probably looked like an okay, albeit strange, family of vegetarians. We believed we were not only special but superior to all others outside of the cult, and those beliefs allowed us to hide the truth from ourselves about who we really were.

CHAPTER TWO

Moving to a New City

I *am seven years old and I cannot believe how lucky I am.*
Our family's moving, and I will not have to go to that yucky
Catholic school anymore. That mean old third-grade nun
will not ever get a chance to shake me! We were moving sixty
miles away to a new town. Dawn and I and eventually the
twins would be going to the "I AM" School.

Looking back upon my childhood environment, there
were so many signs that there was dysfunction in many of the
other families and children we came to know in the school
run by the cult. They, too, had experienced trauma-filled lives.
I met a couple of these children the very first day of school.

On a warm September day in 1958, I walked into a
small room in a white painted stucco house that was now
classrooms. All twelve grades of approximately thirty children
in total attended school in this two-story house. Chalk and
dust tickled my nose. Eight kid-sized desks painted white were
lined up, side by side in two rows for first, second, and third
graders, facing the green chalkboard and a wooden teacher's

desk. We were seated youngest to oldest, so as a third grader, I was in the back.

"Is *dis* your desk?" my red-headed classmate asked in baby-talk.

"I guess so," I replied, hiding my disgust and wondering if he always talked that way. I soon found out that he did. *What a baby!* I thought. *Geez, he is in my grade!*

His first-grade sister who smelled like pee had a desk in front. They lived across the street from the school with their parents who provided room and board during the school year for kids from out-of-town. Everyone referred to their large home as the Residence. *I am sure glad that I do not have to stay in a strange home away from my family like some of the kids.* My little girl self was always comparing how bad I had it and how good I had it. I was jealous of everyone who was getting attention, always sizing things up. *Who's got it best? Who's got it worst?* Their father was a doctor who worked at a VA hospital sixty miles away in the same town as my father still commuted to for work. Their mother had been in a concentration camp and had a number permanently etched on her arm. She spoke with a funny accent.

Monday mornings started in the Assembly Room upstairs. Its large picture window looked out on the green grassy yard. Against the fence I could see bushes that would spill over with lilacs in the spring. Pictures of Ascended Masters and the founders of the "I AM" Activity, Edna and Guy Ballard, looked out at us from the wall. The *All-Seeing Eye of God* was there too. I wondered what it meant. No one ever said. Thirty folding chairs faced a lectern next to a small round table that held candles and a crystal cup. Wearing yellow, the color for Monday, we filed in from youngest to oldest, filling up the rows. The older students usually led the ceremony but occasionally the younger kids were included. I liked being the leader up at the lectern, leading the decrees and songs, calling forth the violet flame to purify us, and lighting candles. The philosophy that continued to imprint me was that being human was an inferior state of being, and we had to guard against the Sinister Force and purify ourselves, so we could become superior like the Ascended Masters, St. Germain and Jesus.

NIGHTTIME DADDY

We are in a new city and this setting not only allows but seems to be ripe for the abuse to continue. I retrieved the following memory during a healing session.

I am seven years old. It is a Sunday evening at the Sanctuary. Daddy looks handsome in his bow tie and brown trousers, and I am happy because he asked me to do something special with him. Even Dawn did not get to come. Daddy says it is just something for me. My daddy says I am special. Daddy needs someone to help with the sound system in the back of the room while he leads the class. I am afraid that I will forget what I am supposed to do, but I manage to flip the switch to play the benediction at the right time. After class, he takes me down to the basement of the Sanctuary. It smells kind of funny. I do not like it here. A sense of dread begins to blanket me as my face become slack and my chest becomes pinched. What are we going to do in this basement? I want to go home now. Daddy gives me a lifesaver. I like lifesavers. As I suck on it, my thoughts scatter, and my head spins. I need to sit down, or I will fall. Daddy brings a wooden horse into the center of the room. I am wobbly with a desperate need to escape, but my arms are limp, and my legs no longer respond to my will. There is no way out. I am engulfed in a wave of helplessness that must be ridden all the way to an evil shore. One of Daddy's hands tightly holds my two together as he bends me over the wooden horse and ties my hands together.

Cold hands spread out my legs. Daddy is tying them down. I become aware of others in the room. It is not just Daddy now.

I cannot make sense of what is happening. Expressing emotion is futile. I just want to leave and never have to remember this stinging betrayal. As he whispers, "go to the light", I surrender my body, and my spirit is welcomed by the angels.

At this time in our lives, my father was away during the entire week and home on weekends. His absentee schedule would continue for subsequent years and so my mother began indulging herself and sometimes her children. She experimented with breaking the rules that had run her life for over three decades. My life became filled with confusion and paranoia about what was okay and what was not okay. The rules kept changing from weekdays to weekends, and I did not know what to expect. Dawn and I noticed that sometimes Mom was like a little girl breaking rules with us. "I made chocolate chip cookies today," she gleefully announced one day on our way home from school.

It is Monday so we will have time to eat them before Daddy comes home Friday evening, I thought. I knew that our father was not to hear of this. "Oh, thank you, thank you, thank you, Mom."

And then there were the swimming lessons. "Please, Mom, pretty please. I really want to learn to swim." Her face twisted with ambivalence. *Maybe she wants me to have some fun. Am I allowed to have swimming lessons? Are they bad? Will we really get contaminated from other people's negative energy in the water like Daddy says?* I was not sure what was safe to do and what was not. Her solution was to find someone in our cult who used a motel pool to give me lessons.

"Yippee, yippee, yippee!" I was bursting with excitement. This everyday activity which was normal for many children was a giant event in my life.

And I wanted to ride a bicycle before I was twelve years old, the age my father had designated as appropriate. I was ten when we secretly broke that rule. *Am I a bad girl for*

21

riding my sister's bike to the grocery store? I also wanted to join Brownies. A neighborhood girl had told me how much fun it was. "Mommy, can I go?"

"No, Honey. It wouldn't be a good idea." My mother would only go so far in breaking the rules, and this was it. I was starting to wonder if *everything* fun was bad.

With the double messages, each experience was tinged with guilt. Permission from my mother was not real permission because it went against my father. Guilt. Every time I had fun and pleasure, I felt guilty.

I was around eight or nine years old when I discovered masturbation. The tingle I felt as we were driving to school was erotic, and I could not resist touching myself as I sat in the backseat of the car. *I will squat on the seat and no one can see what I am doing because I have a coat on.* The fear of being discovered heightened my excitement. As we turned up the hill that approached the school, the intensity of sensation increased as I realized that time was running out. *Oh, this feels so good. Hurry up, hurry up, we are almost at school.* I would climax at the last second, just as we arrived at school. The pleasurable sensations radiated outward, and I felt relaxation enveloping me. *Whew, I did not get caught. That was so nice!* If my mother was ever aware of my self-pleasuring, she did not confront me. Little did I know in the day life that I was being sexually stimulated and abused in the cult at night. I was trained to keep all sexual feelings secret.

The secrecy of the abuse was coupled with shame in the day life by my mother's attitudes. As I look back on the day life, any conversations around sexuality were completely repressed and denied. I recall being fascinated with ads of pictures of women in bras, and I would draw on the magazine to emphasize their breasts even more. "Beth, what did you do to these pictures?" My mother's eyes and tone of voice shot shame into my heart, and I wanted to hide. My mother and

I were trained to stay unconscious and compartmentalized about the sexual experiences and rituals at night. The shame, judgment and rigidity of sexuality was the wall to keep us compartmentalized. In day life, there was no understanding or normal curiosity and exploration of heart-connected sexuality because it did not exist in our family.

The summer that I was eleven, the fifteen-year old babysitter who took care of the kids next door was my source of sex education. I decided to test my mother and see if she would actually tell me what the babysitter had told me. I did not really think she would speak in such detail. "Mom, how are babies made?"

Her response to my inquiry was to borrow a book from her friend that explained how babies were made. I was to read the book. "If you have any questions, let me know," she said in her saccharine sweet voice. *Will she talk about pleasure like the babysitter did? I do not think so.* In sixth grade I decided my mother was a useless source of sexual information.

Pleasure in all forms was always confusing. One time, and one time only, do I remember my father taking us to the A & W Drive-In to get French fries and a root beer float after a family event. Some of the other families were headed that way. "Please, Daddy, we want to go," my sister and I chanted, without real hope of our request being fulfilled.

"Ok," my father responded. We were shocked to hear his "yes". I felt my tummy tighten, listening carefully to the tone of his voice, wondering if I had heard correctly and then fearing he would switch to "no". After all, this was too good to be true. I watched the muscles in his jaw as we drove in silence, afraid that any words might break the magical spell of this wish being granted. For ten minutes our family seemed normal. What blessing from heaven had come upon us? *Maybe there is love here,* I thought as I slurped my root beer float, afraid that it would be swiped from my sticky hands any moment, suspecting it was a trick, and punishment was soon to follow. *How did this happen? Will it ever happen again?* I had no understanding of why he had said yes.

I kept pretending that I really could make good things happen. *You are supposed to make wishes on eyelashes,* I recalled hearing someone say.

I became fascinated with pulling out my eyelashes. I tightened my fingers into pinchers and felt a sense of power as I yanked them out, checking each time to see how many lashes had come out and then blowing them away with a wish.

I wish I could go to the neighborhood carnival at the local school.

I wish I could have ice cream tonight after dinner.

I wish I could go to the State Fair and see the horses.

I wish I could have swimming lessons.

I wish I could ride a bicycle.

I tugged and tugged until my eyes were sore, hardly aware that I had very few lashes left. My eye rims, mostly absent of eyelashes, were swollen and red. At some point, my mother noticed. "Oh Beth, why have you pulled out all your eyelashes?" Her commentary was detached and puzzled, lacking concern, as if a robot had just observed the mid-day news.

There were many other things that she did not notice. Nor did anyone else.

No one ever noticed that I scratched the top of my head, making it bleed until scabs formed, and my fingers became bloody as I picked the scabs again and again.

No one ever noticed that I rocked my legs back and forth every night to soothe myself to sleep.

No one ever noticed my deep attachment to my baby blanket, the one that I scrunched my hand along like a hungry caterpillar inching forward, devouring the cool satin binding, looking for satiation and relief from unnamed fears.

No one ever noticed the courage it took at age seven for me to let my blanket go. My decision. *I am too old for a baby blanket now.*

No one ever noticed that I squeezed my bottom and could not relax in a chair for any period of time.

No one ever noticed that my mom was in a trance, vacant and blank so much of the time.

My comforts were not comforting. They were compensations to stave off the deep terror that ruled my world. There was little focus on play or joy. Obedience and perfection were the rule.

CHAPTER THREE

A Hope for Normal

Apart of myself knew I was seeking normal. Not too long after transferring to our new school, our family began associating with the Adams family. I was infatuated with them. They seemed to have a much better life than my family. I was beginning to see that life could be different. Secretly, I paid attention to the youngest boy who was Dawn's age. *I like his freckles. I wonder if he likes me.*

My Inner Rule Keeper was astonished that Mr. Adams ate bacon and smoked Camel cigarettes. However, I was excited by the fact that my mother was attracted to a family that broke the rules. *What would be in it for me?* Through their mere presence and affluent lifestyle, the Adams family were rabble-rousers envied by many other "I AM" School families.

My mother was now parenting on her own during the week. She spent many evenings with the Adams, leaving us kids at home to fend for ourselves. *Why is Mom always going over to the Adams' house, and we kids are stuck at home? Why does Mom want to go without me?* I was irate and jealous of my mother going to their house, *my* favorite place and people too.

One evening, when I was nine years old, I said to Dawn, "I'm going to hide in the car tonight before Mom leaves for the Adams'. I want to go. It's not fair that Mom always gets to go, and we don't."

"But she'll see you when she gets in the car," Dawn warned.

"No, she won't. I'll be very quiet and hide in the back, so she can't see me."

I snuck out to the garage, got in the back behind the driver's seat and tucked my knees to my chin as I willed myself to be invisible to my mother. My breathing was shallow, and my heart was pounding. I waited. *When is she coming? Am I going to get caught?*

Finally, I heard the door from the house into the garage open. She opened the door of the Kaiser, our second car. I was being very quiet, but I could not stand the suspense any longer.

I stood up. "Oh, my goodness, what are you doing in here?" my mother exclaimed.

"I want to go to the Adams with you. I was going to pop up after you started driving," I said.

"Well, it's a good thing you didn't. You would have given me a mighty scare. I could have wrecked the car when you suddenly appeared."

"Oh," I replied, lowering my head.

"Maybe you can come another time, but tonight is a school night. You need to stay home and go to bed," she chided.

"But it's not fair that you always get to go over there!" I was starved for attention and her denying me this opportunity ignited my anger. I wanted to scream at her, but I did not dare. I was jealous and enraged that she could have something that I could not. *I hate her! She is so mean! She gets all the good stuff. Doesn't she want me to be happy?* Little did I know at the time that Mrs. Adams would die of cancer, and my mother would divorce my father and marry Mr. Adams, uniting our families.

In fifth and sixth grades, I often had fantasies of receiving love and attention from the older girls at the school. I pictured myself standing by the lockers that they used. I would be crying and one or two of them would run over to comfort me. *What's wrong Beth? You are so cute and special. Why don't you come and sit with us?* They would then hug me, and I would momentarily forget my loneliness and feel like I was loved. This imaginary vision kept me going although it never happened. It never crossed my mind to share my feelings or expose my secret desperation. These feelings were normal, and I did not question them. Instead, I focused on wanting to grow up soon so I could wear make-up and be beautiful and admired. When I was occasionally included to fill in as a partner in the after-school dance class for the older girls, I slurped up the attention and pumped myself up with feelings of superiority. *I am very special because the teacher picked me to dance with the older girls, and I am good enough to quickly learn the steps. I am more special than the other little girls.* My inner world was filled with two extremes: thoughts of arrogance, specialness and superiority contrasted by a desperate desire to be invisible and die.

I knew the older boys thought I was cute. Their playful teasing made me very self-conscious as I would scurry through the school exit door where one or more of them would be standing. My skin would start to tingle, and blood would rush to my head. *Is that Ken who is looking at me right now?* I had a generic crush on all the boys, regardless of their age. In the milieu of sexual feelings and attraction being shameful, every "I AM" School student seemed determined to pair up with someone. My fifth-grade boyfriend was Paul who would carry my books to the car when I got picked up after school. *Wow! I have a boyfriend. I am special.*

Developing childhood friends and activities was limited to mainly those in the School and neighbor children on occasion. "People in the Outer World just don't have the understandings that we do," my mother proclaimed. My father preferred that we stick around home on the weekends. We did chores, sometimes attended the Saturday afternoon Violet Flame class, went to Sunday School, and only sometimes were allowed to play with a friend.

Every once in a while, the hope for normal became a reality. I received roller skates for Christmas the year I was ten. At last, a sanctioned occasion to leave the house! I put my roller skates on and tightened them with my key. I was ready for flight. *I can go all the way around the block! That is not too far for me!* I pushed forward, slow at first, legs in tandem motion, arms thrusting steadily, building momentum, elevating my spirit within. My speed increased until I was pumping as hard as I was able. I could hardly believe how easily I negotiated the bumps on the sidewalk and the turns at the corners. I was completely in the present moment. I could be nowhere else. *I am free. I am free. I can do it!* I sensed a force greater than myself supporting my journey. It was no longer just hope for normal, I had grabbed an experience of freedom that was mine, and I could experience it over and over. I know now that the freedom on my roller skates was my connection to my inner spiritual strength and perseverance to not only endure and stay alive but to know that I, no matter what, deserved to be a free and loved being.

CHAPTER FOUR

Nighttime Normal

At the age of twelve, the suppressed shame of my nightlife turned into feelings of disgust during the day. I look in the mirror. My eyes pierce the image before me. A round face with buck teeth and a gap between them stares back at me. The pointy little bumps that are supposed to be breasts disgust me. *How pathetic!* My eyes move to my waistline. My pleated skirt adds girth emphasizing my pudgy belly. I look away quickly, ashamed of what I see.

I am momentarily distracted by the shiny gold chain necklace that adorns my chest. I practice a pretty, sweet smile to present to others. "Hello, how are you doing?" I rehearse a friendly tone and a competent demeanor, pretending that I feel fine, pretending, like my mother does. My emotions fade to numb. I tell myself that I feel happy as I shove the waves of shame and grief beneath the surface of my mind, hiding the emotion under the skin of my placid face.

BRIDE OF THE ANTI-CHRIST

My intense feelings of helplessness, stupidity, and worthlessness were the fertile ground in my psyche to prepare me for the ceremony that would give me a taste of power and a sense of importance. In 2016, I retrieved the memory of becoming the bride of the Anti-Christ at the age of twelve.

The participants are wearing masks. I, too, have been given a devil's mask. The sight and smell of the ceremony, along with the mask that they hand me, brings an alter (a personality compartmentalized and separate from my conscious self) forward.

Chanting and high-pitched cackling fill the ceremonial room. Faces of the other participants hide behind grotesque masks, and the smell of incense fills the chamber. I am drugged with something that makes me malleable to their control. I look at the array of instruments laid out on a metal stand: knives, sticks, pliers, crosses; I suck in my breath, stealing barely enough oxygen to satisfy my lungs.

Now that I am twelve, the women prepare me to become the Bride of the Anti-Christ. I am clothed in a ceremonial gown. "This white gown represents your purity. You are the special one, the virgin bride. You are the chosen one. We celebrate you. We will call forth the Anti-Christ, so you can give yourself to Him. He will enter you. We will show you how the woman is the special one. You have the power to claim His power in you. All you must do is open your legs and let this animal tickle you. It shows you the pleasure of your body." A snake is writhing between my legs. I realize that I am to receive the snake inside me.

My mother is behind one of the masks. She leans back and cackles while stimulating herself, showing me what I am to do. "It is your time now. We are going to show you how to be the bride."

I am alarmed as I look at my mother. My mother is not my mother. (I now understand that she was in her alter personality.)

31

She is caught up in a frenzy of rhythms, chants, and drumming. She is smiling, and I think she looks like she is proud of her role and proud that her daughter is about to receive special powers. She urges me to comply. I am terrified of what will happen if I disobey: she could be punished, I could be punished or killed. I must submit. I am in an altered drugged state, entranced with the snake; it is as if the snake and I are one.

The group of women lead me to the ceremonial altar at the center of the circle. "You get to perform the sacrifice so the blood can bring the Anti-Christ. We will invoke Him through this sacrifice. You have the power. You have the power. You have the power. Show us your power. Invoke the Anti-Christ through your sacrifice." They begin to chant "Beelzebub, Beelzebub, Beelzebub" and I feel Beelzebub enter me and consume my body and psyche. I am possessed and an alter in me comes forth. This alter feels a surge of rage as adrenaline rushes through her body. Another part of my awareness is outside of my body watching the whole thing. I have been split into many parts. A knife is put into my twelve-year old hand. Who is in charge of this hand? I feel pressure to kill and slaughter or die myself. I close my eyes and surrender to the frenetic force inside of me, no longer in choice. I am trembling with excitement and fear. The chanting sounds and the cackling shrill of my mother's voice fill my head as my alter reaches for the knife and pliers, ready to dismember the baby on the altar. My hand descends into the heart of the boy baby and I pause to insert the cross into his chest, followed by continual thrusts of the blade. After the child is sacrificed, the feast of flesh and blood begins. The satanic energies, now one with my twelve-year old, feed off the flesh and I have joined with the Anti-Christ. I feel a sense of elation and a high like no other. I am no longer powerless. I feel invincible. I have surrendered into this dark power.

I could not bear to witness any of this until I had been uncovering memories for thirteen years. This soul retrieval session allowed me to release the satanic spirits so I could heal my body of the mind control and alter personality that emerged during the rituals. I will explain in Chapter Eighteen how this alter personality was reprogrammed and integrated into my conscious awareness.

Through the process of regaining this memory, I understood now why I was the way I was during my elementary school years and at twelve, filled with self-hatred and sexual shame. I was terrified of sex. During my day life, I was out of my body most of the time and dissociated totally from my feelings. There was no way to report what was going on in my home because everything was buried so deeply inside of me. With the surfacing of these memories, I finally had compassion for the terrified, traumatized young girl that I was who could find no place of love or safety in this world.

CHAPTER FIVE

Shattered Hope

As I had hoped for a better life, my fantasy finally became true at thirteen. My mother took me to the Adams' house where she was housesitting and sat me down in a chair. "I'm divorcing your father and going to marry Mr. Adams. It will be wonderful. Now we will be able to go as a family to the Ice Capades."

That news landed like a punch in my gut, followed by uncontrollable sobs. Until now, I had presented a happy face no matter what was happening in my family. My mother was surprised at the level of emotion I expressed, and so was I. Such shocking news of my parents' divorce broke through my façade. *Poor Daddy. It is all my fault because I wanted to become an Adams.*

Edna Ballard, who we called Beloved Mama, sent word via the school principal through us kids to my mother and stepfather-to-be that their marriage was not sanctioned by St. Germain. The whole school bowed to the authority of this spirit being who was considered the superior authority that

34

knew what was best for everyone. Thus, we finished out the school year at the "I AM" School and began public school in the Fall. I perceived that my life was finally going to change for the better.

GOING TO PUBLIC SCHOOL

The year was 1964. As I stepped on the school bus, I took the first empty seat, avoiding eye contact. *Was I now one of the Outer World people?* My mind began to race. *What if I breathe the same air as everybody else? Will I be affected by their energy? I am not a normal human. I am special. These kids are so unruly, mouthy, stupid, and immature.* I kept my eyes straight ahead. I just wanted to fit in and not be noticed. I tried to be invisible.

I knew my top priority was to be the best, smartest student and please the teachers. I was surprised to discover that, in spite of having gone to such a small school, I was more than able to compete academically in the public school. And while I looked at everyone as being beneath me, I had no idea how to fit into this Outer World, so I began to imitate what I saw. With hypervigilance I observed other students' gestures, the movement in their eyebrows, their tone of voice. I applied my practiced smile and nonchalant voice so I could look casual and normal. *Hi. How is it going?* There were few spontaneous smiles because I kept a rigid grip on my image. Nothing came natural to me.

One of my favorite classes was choir. I entered the room and sat in my assigned seat as a soprano. *I can read music. I know how to sing and follow the notes.* My voice got louder, and my heart felt a pitter patter of joy as we sang "Climb Every Mountain". I did not exactly know what my dream was, but the very idea that a dream could be entertained uplifted me. I had hope for something undefined, something that felt magical. *I love music! I wish I could sing all day!* By the end of the day, I was in my Home Economics class, eager to show off my competence. Would we bake brownies or sew a jumper? I looked at my classmates. *They do not catch on very fast.* I patiently and carefully watched the teacher's demonstration and then got down to business. *Yes! I am good at this stuff!* I was so excited about sewing that I started making clothes for myself at home.

Some of the Hispanic boys thought I was cute and talked to me. I froze when they came around. *What am I supposed to say to them? They are off limits to me because I would never date anyone beneath me.* I tried to act friendly by saying hello, but I really wanted to retreat and become invisible. And yet, I liked the attention because it made me feel like I mattered, even though I felt totally out of place. Seeing my name in the school newsletter helped me pretend that I fit in with my classmates. As I look back now, I realize that I was leaving my body, hovering above the social situations, escaping the intense feelings of terror that being around other people and especially boys produced.

The following year I can see my ego stepping in. I felt grown up and "cool" when I went with a couple of girls off campus at lunchtime for frito pies at the nearby Woolworth's. I did not talk about my former school experiences. Those were best left behind. Every so often on the weekends I spent the night with a girlfriend, but I mostly preferred staying at home.

I convinced myself that I was fitting in. Though I relied on imitation of others and false friendliness, I was experiencing moments of joy in choir reminiscent of the roller-skating high. And I was developing a sense of confidence that I could be in the Outer World by gaining practical skills like sewing and baking.

The material side of my day life did improve with my mother's remarriage. I got a new wardrobe for the school year, began sneaking ice cream out of the basement freezer, and watched The Beatles perform on the Ed Sullivan Show in 1965. I started eating meat which seemed natural to me, and I was now free to wear red and black. My mother started to drink alcohol for the first time in her life, joining my stepfather with a cocktail. *Why is it now okay to wear red and black? Were we "right" when we were in the "I AM" or are we "right" now that we no longer follow their rules?* I had little understanding of what I liked because my concern was always honed on choosing what was considered "right" by the current authority.

Daily life required adjustments with my mother's remarriage. On a practical level, we doubled up in the bedrooms to make room for my stepbrother and stepsister. I inherited five stepsiblings, with two living in the blended home.

THE "HAPPY FAMILY"

My mother's fantasy of a happy family life did not last long. There was competition, jealousy, and plenty of tension in the house. Everyone was emotionally detached and flat and could not express how awful they felt. There was no honesty. We were supposed to be siblings, but we were just a family of familiar strangers.

Mr. Adams, who we now called "Dad", was a new authority in my life. Obedience was still the top priority. I generally never spoke up to my stepfather. However, my spiritual desire for free expression surprised me one weekend afternoon when we six kids were called into the living room for a family meeting. What that meant was Dad would lay down some rules or corrections for our behavior in his usual intimidating manner. He would talk. We would listen. My mother sat quietly to the side. When we were settled and looking at him, he began to tell us about what he would and would not put up with. "Make sure your laundry is in the hamper or it's not going to get washed." *No problem for me. I always use my hamper.* "There's no eating in the living room." *What a silly rule. I never make a mess.* And, "you guys need to be in bed by 10:00 on school nights." *When is he going to be done prattling on about these ridiculous rules?* At some point he asked, "Do you understand?"

My mind was racing. *He is so stupid. He does not even realize that I would never cause any trouble for him. I do not need this lecture. What a bastard.* My suppressed rage bubbled up. I blurted, "Yes, I *understand* but that doesn't mean that I agree with you." I received silence.

Upon reflection, my emotional outbursts surprised me as much as anybody else. I had no inner awareness of why I felt what I felt. I recall feeling nothing about my birth father after the initial shock of learning of the divorce. By the age of thirteen, I did not miss him. It was as if he had been erased from my life. No emotion. No longing. I was numb. I had deposited everything related to him in a box labeled *Untouchable.* I had no attachment to him and felt no loss. I was fully on board with my mother's fantasy that we were now in a wonderful, new life, and I easily replaced my father with a stepfather. We had gained status by entering a moderately wealthy family and had lots of distractions to keep us from dealing with the pain of the truth of our lives.

Thus, I did not mind when, a year later, my mother asked us children to write my father a letter requesting that we be adopted by our stepfather. "You kids are very irritable when you come back from visits with your father. This will be so much better for you," my mother had said. It seemed like a fine idea. My father became dead to me. His presence no longer entered my mind, especially after he consented to the adoption. It was only when I became a parent myself that I recognized the magnitude of his decision to release his parental rights to four children. Upon reflection as an adult, I am aware that allowing our adoption meant he no longer had to pay child support which would be a big financial relief to this man of moderate means. It is clear that he was as detached to any real bonding to us as we were to him. Later in life, I noted that I continued to relate to men with this cold, robotic demeanor, repeating the dynamic that I knew with my father.

An Unwelcome Visitor

My hope that my new father was different from my old father quickly unraveled at the age of fourteen. This is not a retrieved memory but is a conscious memory that I have carried with me about my experience with my new family.

I awakened one night from a very deep sleep. I was not sure why I had awakened, and I was shocked to realize that someone was sitting at the foot of my bed on the floor. *What is happening? Am I asleep? Am I dreaming?* I asked myself.

Fear took hold and I did not dare move. My breathing became shallow, and I willed my chest to be still. A programmed response took over. *Please, do not let anything be happening,* I pleaded to the dark night. *If someone is here, do not let them know that you are awake. Be invisible. Be quiet. Pretend it is not happening. Go back to sleep.*

The next morning, I felt very confused. I simply could not allow this terrifying intrusion to be real. *I imagined this. I am making it up.* I paused to consider. *Had something happened in the middle the night? No one else is aware of a disturbance so I do not want to mention it and get others upset.* I had no recall of the nighttime rituals that had happened up until this age. My conscious fourteen-year old thoughts were to downplay what had happened, just as I had been trained to do during my nighttime programming. *I will not say anything to Mom. I certainly do not want to be the cause of a problem.* I was trained to be silent, to pretend I was invisible, to talk myself out of my experiences being real or that they ever happened. I was trained not to tell no matter what. As this event repeated itself, I finally began locking my bedroom door. I later discovered through retrieved memory that it was my stepfather entering my bedroom.

In 2010, through memory retrieval, I learned about the continuation of violence that my fourteen-year old experienced during rituals in my new family.

I am being led down a dark, dank hallway. The air is heavy and filled with odors that are stale. As we enter a room, the air becomes warmer, and incense fills my nose. A low hum permeates the large chamber. Someone has rubbed oil on my body painting symbols that are intersecting Vs. Men are naked and gathered in a circle, bent down on spread knees, facing outward with heads resting on the concrete floor, genitals hanging below the aperture between their cheeks. I am in the center of the gathering. They have removed my robe and I am naked. My body is swaying, undulating, drugged and out-of-focus, moving in a fog. I am handed a whip. A man's hands signal me which triggers an alter to come forth. This alter wields the whip, instructed to tease the men, inflict pain, and excite and incite them. My alter knows what to do. She is the initiator of the seeds that are collected into the urn; they tell me that this is a collection of life force to be gathered from the males for the glory of Satan. I feel power and excitement surge through my loins. I begin to whip the men as they bow to my power with their howls of pain and pleasure, and a hideous laughter is emitted from their throats. They masturbate themselves and each other as the chanting builds in volume and intensity, moving toward its own climax as they make their contribution into the urn. I am directed to drink from the urn as a symbol of the fertility of the men being celebrated. My stepfather is there. He fondles my breasts as he tells me I have done a good job.

When I retrieved this memory and integrated it, my conscious self wanted to vomit. My compassion, as an adult, increased for my cold mistrust of all men and my self-hatred. With this continuing in my night life, I remained isolated from friends and family and had no expectation that life could be fulfilling. In Chapter Seventeen, I will discuss more of the healing process in reclaiming my alters.

NO BUFFERS

When I was fifteen, my stepbrother and Dawn were out of the house, off to college. It was now just me and the twins. I remember feeling that my buffers had disappeared, and I was truly alone to navigate my mother's relationship with my stepfather.

One evening, I heard my mother say, "Don't you think you've had enough, Bill? Why don't you put the bottle away?" Her voice was strained, trying to sound pleasant. I felt my gut tighten with the familiar sensation of helplessness and fear.

"There's nothing wrong with alcohol, you know. That is, unless you want to go back to your old life." Dad was beginning to slur words and was becoming belligerent. "Just leave me alone, Woman," he mumbled, brushing off her request.

As I hustled up the stairs to find out what was happening, my mother ran into her bedroom. Seeing a suitcase on the bed behind my mother alarmed me. "Wh... What are you doing?" I muttered. My mother yanked her dresser drawer open and was pulling clothes out. Adrenaline was pumping through my veins at the thought that my mother might be leaving the house.

"I can't stay in the house with him this way." Her voice quivered as she tilted her head toward the living room where he sat with his scotch. "I'm going to a motel."

"Please, Mom, don't go," I begged as tears flowed down my cheeks. *Can she hear me? Does she care about me? Obviously not.* "You can't leave me here," I cried. "Please let me come with you." But I immediately knew I could not leave my younger brother and sister behind. But *she* could.

My mother was so detached from the consequences of her actions that I never felt safe with her. Neither were my brother and sister safe, and I never knew what would happen next. Thankfully, she did not leave the house that night.

PLEASE GOD, HELP ME

Throughout my teen years, there were glimpses of my spiritual desire for connection to something greater. The ecstasy of roller skating continued to be an imprint of freedom that sparked again at fourteen when I felt joy through singing. At sixteen, I had an experience of wonderment and grandeur beneath the nighttime sky. I remember looking up at the stars and feeling a sense of connection to something greater than myself. I was very upset, scared, and sad, and I did not know why. Amidst the vast expanse of twinkling stars, I felt the contradiction of my insignificance *and* significance in all of it. Tears ran down my face as I realized I had been at this same emotional cliff before. I wanted to die.

Please God, I feel so awful. Help me. I do not know what to do. If there really is a God, You will help me. I do not see how this can get better, but if it does, I will know for sure that You exist.

By the next morning, as if I were a different person, I would feel better. I had switched parts. In my healing work I discovered I had many personalities and parts that had different jobs that I will discuss in Chapters Seventeen and Eighteen. My life would feel manageable, even fine, and I would wonder why I had been upset. I now understand my compartmentalized psyche could not make sense of my deep despair. Wanting to forget the pain, I would go back to my robotized life of following the rules, hoping that the moments of desolation were gone for good. Of course, they were not.

In later years, through soul retrieval and its accompanying memories, I discovered that both my biological father and my stepfather were part of some of the same satanic rituals. As an adult, I can see that my mother had simply moved from one abuser to another. The cult that we had departed from had connections with the satanic activities of the Freemasonry system that my stepfather was in. Our adoption by my stepfather seemed to be a show of power over my biological father which makes me suspect that he, my stepfather, had moved up in rank in the cult hierarchy and, thereafter, had more authority to influence what happened with my siblings and me. In my research later in life, I discovered that many organizations that do satanic worship share the ritualized, abused children.

CHAPTER SIX

Following the Plan

I was sitting in the living room watching Johnny Carson. My stepsister offered me some nuts. *No thank you. I will just have a glass of orange juice.* A surge of strength filled my veins. *I have power over my body, at last.* I wanted the power that I saw in skinny, beautiful women. I pored over calorie counting charts memorizing those evil numbers that could wreck my figure. *I want an ice cream cone, so I will skip the hamburger.* For years I yo-yo dieted and denied myself well-balanced nutrition. Especially at sixteen, I was hypervigilant about my intake of food.

Bear asked me out. He was my first boyfriend. He met the requirements. He was a white Anglo Saxon protestant and knew how to be polite. He was into sports and drove an old white Cadillac. I wore his class ring on a chain around my neck because we were going steady. This was a vanilla, socially acceptable, perfect relationship. *I do not know if I am attracted to him, but I am proud that there is a boy interested in me. I feel important when I sit in the front seat of the Cadillac with Bear.*

44

Then I met Terry who was tall and wiry with reddish blonde hair. His father was an alcoholic, and he lived only with his mother. I was flattered by his pursuit of me. One day I heard him bark to his mother, "Hey Bitch, what's the matter with you?" I cringed in a moment of self-awareness. *What kind of guy is this? What am I doing with someone so rude?* We had plans to go to the senior prom. *I guess I am normal, I am going to the Prom.* After dinner and dancing on Prom night, we headed up to the mountains with a bottle of champagne to celebrate our soon-to-be-completed high school year and my honor of being valedictorian. I started feeling the effects of the champagne as my shoulders began to drop. I leaned against Terry, he started kissing me passionately, and his hands started finding places down my body. I reached into his pants. Suddenly my hand was filled with something wet and sticky. Ug! I was immediately triggered and flooded with shame and disgust. I withdrew, going silent and rigid. "Take me home," I whispered. I felt like I was trapped in the car and could not get away from the mess fast enough.

Through my healing work, I have come to understand that the buried memories of sexual distortion from the nighttime rituals made me frigid and terrified of sex. Sexual energy did not mean pleasure and affection. It meant violence and degradation.

THE COLLEGE YEARS

In 1968, I headed to college in a town five-hundred miles from my home. I started to feel different, a little freer. I now realize that this began a time where I was not being taken consistently to rituals. In my new environment, I was excited to direct many aspects of my life. I could choose my classes and schedule; I could walk downtown and shop; I could attend a college party and drink sloe gin; I could say "yes" or "no" when asked for a date; I could drink 3.2 beer after turning eighteen my freshman year; I could go to my roommate's home for the week-end. I had options, and it felt good. My goal was to become an elementary school teacher, and I was eager to have some fun.

I had decided to become a schoolteacher around the time I was eight. I had conscious memory of the cruel nun who made me go without any underwear after I had accidentally wet my pants in first grade. *I will not be like her! I will be kind to children who are having difficulties.* I wanted to become a teacher so that I could rescue and help children. Also, from my childish, powerless perspective, I yearned to be the one in charge. *When I am the teacher, I will have a great life. I will always be in charge!* At last, I would be in control of my life.

In my sophomore and junior years, I grew in confidence. I could talk to my roommates and felt cared for. I returned those positive feelings. We went out to eat on occasion, shared chores in the apartment, and I began to open to friendship. Jackie and I were philosophers. Sometimes we would meet on Friday afternoons at the college hang-out to have a beer and gab about what we thought life was about. "I think it's the little things in life that mean the most," I declared, "like eating dinner together. It's important to have fun, otherwise life becomes very dull."

"I have found that to be true," Jackie nodded as I watched her eyes sparkle. "My little secret to being with my guy is to leave little surprise notes in one of his textbooks. It's such a small thing but then he knows that I am thinking about him." My heart felt warm as I gazed at Jackie. I felt closer to her than the other roommates because she was easy to talk to, and she usually validated my point of view. *Wow! She even seems to think I am okay.*

In our small group we took turns cooking dinner. We would laugh at mealtimes. "Where is Pa?" one of us joked.

46

"He run off one day. Now don't you worry 'bout it," another responded with a hillbilly accent. I enjoyed the camaraderie even though I still did not feel free to divulge the strange religious group I had been raised in. I felt a little more normal because of these friendships.

I slowly gained a greater sense of belonging as I developed new relationships and the skills needed to live as an adult in the world. My front personality (the day to day part that was conscious and aware of itself) was high functioning, and no one could detect anything but an obedient, pretty, sweet, friendly yet shy, achievement-oriented young woman. I was completely unaware of the programmed aspects that were the diabolical opposite of my front personality.

I AM A TEACHER

It was January 1972, and I had just turned twenty-one. I stared out at twenty-five fourth-graders, hesitant to take charge. *I have my lesson plans, but I am not sure anybody is listening.* Because I was ashamed to admit that I did not know everything, I could not ask for help from my supervising teacher. I had such little capacity to hold boundaries that she sometimes stepped in anyway. With her coaching, I said in my most-adult voice, "Jimmy, go sit down in your seat. Do not get up to sharpen your pencil without permission."

I was attracted to the school counselor, Ed. It was my first real attraction to a man. *How am I going to stay focused on my teaching with him around? I have never felt like this before.* I became extremely self-conscious around him as my attraction to him grew. My legs would begin to quiver as I walked past his office. One day while I was teaching class, he came in, interrupted the class, pretended to have business with me, and then quietly mumbled, "Would you like to go out to dinner this evening?" I suppressed my excitement and the grin that wanted to break out around my mouth. I nodded yes. I dared not let the students see my attraction to the counselor. *Oh, I think Ed is going to be 'the One'. Maybe I am lovable after all.* I was allowing myself to feel good, to feel sexual and affectionate.

Our sexual relationship developed very slowly. I was ambivalent, to say the least. I remember saying to myself, *I want the decision to have sex to be made on purpose. I do not want to just give in to the heat of passion and regret it later. I need to choose what I really want.* I see now that I was afraid that a part of me would take over and "give in". When I was away from Ed, I could have the intention to "not go too far" with sex and then change my mind when we were together. I am now aware of the divergent voices inside of me. *I want to have sex. I want to be close to him.* And yet as I lay on the bed, another part of me was ashamed, rigid, and judging. *Do not look at me. Do not bother me with your desires. I do not want to have sex. I do not feel like it.* I unconsciously anticipated violation. My arms closed across my chest. My breath was short. *But maybe I should. It is normal. After all, neither of us are dating anyone else.*

I was still wrestling with rigidity and frigidity but part of me desired something more. I wanted to love and be loved, even if I did not know how. I was beginning to trust Ed, and eventually I allowed intercourse.

I later learned in session work that my sexual repression and confusion prevented me from truly bonding with Ed. It was as if I had a ten-thousand-pound wet blanket of shame smothering my connection to him.

Graduation day was a beautiful, spring day with blossoms budding on the trees and tulips pushing up out of the ground. My parents drove out for the occasion. I was proud to introduce them to Ed, such a handsome man, almost ten years my senior who had an affable demeanor. We stood together underneath the budding green of a cottonwood, and my mother snapped a photo of the two of us. I am beaming in my cap and gown, my long, sunlit light brown hair framing my smile, and Ed looking dapper in his linen sports jacket. She smiled at Ed and then at me. It was as if I could read her thoughts. *You two will make a fine couple.* I take in her approval. *I am hoping that Ed sees it that way too.*

"We need to know each other at least six months before we move forward," Ed tells me. He does not even want to say the word *marriage. I* want to get married, but I realize that his request is reasonable. *I will feel safe and secure once he proposes. What on earth will I do if he does not want to marry me?* Mom and Dad offer a trip to France as my graduation gift. After all, I have always wanted to go. Not anymore. *I do not want to leave Ed. I will pass up France and just take money instead. If I leave, Ed may be gone when I get back.*

That summer, Ed took me to his hometown to meet his parents. I led with my sunniest smile and brightest voice. "Can I help with the dishes? Oh, what a beautiful dress you have on." Our visit spanned three days, and soon we said our good-byes. I noted the tears that his mother was trying to hide. She did not want us to go. *I think I am going to have more family soon. I hope so.* I was starting to feel the pleasure of being wanted by a new family.

As we drove home Ed mentioned that we were approaching our six-month mark of being together, and then he started talking about shopping for wedding rings. I breathed a deep sigh of relief and an aura of contentment enveloped me. *I no longer need to worry about Ed abandoning me. He must really love me.* It was not a romantic proposal, but it was enough for me.

My life was following the plan. I had been hired for a full-time teaching job with fifth graders at the same school where I had been a student teacher, and I was engaged to be married. It never occurred to me that there might be other choices. I could not imagine anything else. I felt safe, knowing I would have Ed to rely on. Everything looked perfect.

The family secrets would remain hidden as I followed what I thought was the path for a happy life.

CHAPTER SEVEN

Learning to Bond

The year was 1972. I was twenty-one years old and starting my new teaching job. It was as if I was having an initiation into human connection for the very first time. I strutted down the hallway with pride wearing the label, "Ed's Fiancée". In my first teaching job of fifth graders, I had such a mix of kids. Like all fifth-grade classes, there were several snotty, snarky girls in my classroom who ogled over Ed, and when one of the mothers told me her daughter was jealous, I was shocked. I had such little understanding of emotional dynamics.

There were others that my heart went out to like Christine. *She almost never speaks. I am afraid if I look at her the wrong way, she will crumble. You do not have to speak if you do not want to, but I see you.* I knew her place of invisibility and mute silence so well. Then there was Carla who could not memorize her multiplication tables no matter how hard she tried. Her plain face with the crooked teeth and dirty hair stared into empty space much of the time. The school social

51

worker made consistent visits to her home. *I wonder if she knows I care.* I got special permission to bring her to my apartment after school to make popcorn balls for our class for Halloween. She was an abandoned child.

I was surprised by Martin. "Here you go. Me and the other kids got you these flowers for Valentine's Day." I smiled at him as he handed me a bouquet of red and white carnations. Here was the kid who had thrown his brownie in the cafeteria and made it stick to the ceiling. I could not remain annoyed with him now.

"Thank you," I responded. I felt warm inside. I experienced sensations in my heart that I now understand to be bonding. These were new to me. *I want to love these children and let them know they are cared for.*

I hoped I could make a positive impact on some of these lives. Much later in self-reflection, I realized that I was a master detector of abused and needy children who were mirroring my own battered parts, even though I only thought of myself as a sensitive and caring teacher at the time.

I am so excited to get married. I have just turned twenty-two, and I am going home to have a church wedding. *Mom has spent endless hours in the planning, and I know everything will be perfect. She knows how to create beautiful social occasions. I cannot wait to be married.* I want to please my husband. I never go out without make-up, and I weigh myself daily. One time, Ed asked me how much I weighed. My stomach tightened and I sucked my tummy in immediately. "Well, what would be good?" I asked defensively. "Is 110 pounds okay?" *I just need to lose another five pounds and then I will be perfect. I will keep better track of my calories this week.* I also tracked every penny spent at the grocery store. Ed was big on saving money. On the weekends I cleaned our duplex and did laundry. If it was early in the month and we were still within our budget, we might eat out or have a couple of our teacher friends over.

Our sex life was a time of learning about each other. In the very early days of consciously exploring sex, there was a part of me that I will call the Little Girl, who would often be in bed with Ed. *What is Ed going to do? Should I take my clothes off? I feel more aroused when my clothes are on and we slowly remove them.* As I regressed into my child self, I was mute, compliant, and numb. Shame engulfed me and I was not able to tell Ed what was pleasurable for me. I knew I was able to have orgasms because I had been masturbating since the age of eight which I had told no one about, even in college. It was shameful to me to even speak of being aroused. We were married for a year before I was able to bring it up.

And then there was my tiger part where all I wanted was to feel in control and dominant. When I was in this state my eyes would glaze over and I remember thinking, *I just want to screw.* It did not matter to me how he felt.

My interest in sex was unpredictable. There were times when I had no interest. I recall lying in bed next to Ed. "Let's have sex," he says.

"OK." *I am not really in the mood, but I cannot say no. He might not love me if I do not have sex with him. His eyes are closed. He is not saying anything. I get the impression he is relaxing and tuning in to himself and his desires.* I am impatient and irritated with the whole thing. I push my resentment down. *I am supposed to want this. Having an orgasm does not happen easily for me. I will probably just end up feeling frustrated. What is he waiting for? I need to clean the bathrooms this afternoon. Let's just get it over with. I feel guilty for not wanting to have sex, but I do not want to say anything. I feel trapped and angry and want to bolt out of bed, but I cannot move.* Never, in all my time with Ed, did I tell him how I felt about sex. I could only pretend that everything was fine.

On the occasion when I did feel connected to Ed, I always felt a deep well of sadness as I lay on his chest after he orgasmed. My heart felt broken and I wanted to sob, but I could not. As I write this now as a sixty-eight-year-old woman, I know my twenty-four-year old self was longing for healing. I was starting to defrost.

HOW CAN I GIVE WHAT I DO NOT HAVE?

Ed and I always talked about having children. After five years we decided we were as ready as we would ever be, and I became pregnant. The day I told Ed I was pregnant, he slowly looked at me without changing expression and said, "That's great. It's good that we have been practicing living off one salary so now we are prepared to be pregnant." I sat there in silence wondering what I should be feeling. *Is he happy? Am I happy? Oh my God, how am I going to know what to do with a baby? Ed says he wants to have a child, but I wonder if he really means it. How big will I get? How long is it going to take me to get my figure back? Am I going to know how to be a mother? I am sure I can find some books to read about all of this.*

My normally numb body started to tingle, ache, and open in brand new places. With every passing week I had more and more awareness of myself. My belly continually felt heavy, slightly crampy, as if I were going to start my period any moment. I felt increasing, inner pressure of the growing human inside me. I never even considered talking to my growing baby.

Steven was born in 1978. As I am bringing him home from the hospital, everything outside looks different. I see light around the trees, and the leaves look like they are dancing. Everything is sparkling and seems super alive with an enchanted quality about it. My arms are tingling, and I feel a warm flow throughout my body, gently pulsing through my arms and legs. Life feels new and expansive. *I feel new. Has the world really changed or is it just my imagination? Something has slipped into the space between each moment.* I whisper sweet words to my baby. "I love you, Little One. Thank you for coming into my life."

Time had rearranged itself and was now infused with a depth and breadth that was fuller than I had ever experienced before. Something beautiful had been birthed inside me when my son came into the world.

WHO AM I NOW?

Nothing in my life had prepared me for the tidal wave of confusion and emotions I felt as I tried to bond with my new son.

It is Sunday afternoon and Steven has been home from the hospital for a few days. He is napping while Ed is watching the football game in the living room. I hear Steven's cries. My body tenses. *Baby's awake. Back on duty. I do not know if I can take the crying.* A ball of fear and frustration is held in by every rigid muscle in my body. *What am I supposed to do with this endlessly crying child? I am so frustrated I want to scream. But that would mean something is wrong and it is not, because I love my baby. What am I going to do?* I open the door to his bedroom and gently lift him from his crib. *Time to nurse. That will quiet him down.* As I settle on the couch, a surge of energy moves through my solar plexus and I imagine throwing him across the room. *Oh my God! I cannot do that!* My head starts to ache with a piercing pain as Steven attaches to my breast. I close my eyes. I fall asleep looking for relief. I wake up and remember the impulse. *What happened? Did I stop myself? I guess I did. I am still sitting here. Thank God he is not screaming right now. I better not tell Ed.*

Throughout the next few months, I had surges of frustration and desperation that I never spoke about. *I feel so angry. I wish I could throw a set of dishes against the wall and hear them shatter. Better not. I would just waste dishes and have a big mess to clean up.* I rarely left the house. I was living in a fog of baby feedings, loads of laundry, and naps. My life was not my own. Would things ever be normal?

Ed is sitting at the dining table, just having finished his daily breakfast of raisin bran. I put my arms around him and snuggle up in a suggestive way.

"Whoa! You really need to brush your teeth," Ed remarks. I immediately feel rejected, disgusted with myself, and deep shame. *I am ugly. He does not want me.*

Rarely would I ask Ed for help; I worried more about what he needed. I was terrified he might abandon me in my needy state, so I hid my feelings well. I did not want to go back to work. *I cannot handle both teaching and taking care of Steven and our home.* Ed went along with my decision.

When Steven was six months old, I came out of isolation and formed a mother's support group with a friend which we called Mothers Are People Too. I started feeling some empathy for the challenges of being a new mom. *It is hard to be a mom but connecting with other mothers helps.* I saw my own mother twice a year, but she offered little grand mothering to my son; her way of connecting was to buy fancy outfits for him from time to time. Upon opening these gifts, I would become enraged, disgusted, and judgmental. I felt guilty that I did not appreciate my mother's efforts. Little did I know that my rage about these clothes was displaced emotion from my own deep betrayal with her.

Childcare for a couple mornings a week became a priority for me. Yoga, shopping, reading, meditation. I tried to find activities that helped me feel calm. *Maybe I will try making a cassette tape with positive suggestions on it so I can program myself to create what I want.*

I was always looking for my next book. A good friend introduced me to *The Seth Material*. "Here," she said, handing me a tidy paperback. "You might enjoy this." As I began reading, my mind became focused as I shut out the world and entered into an almost hypnotic state. *I cannot put this down. Here it is in black and white, the most comprehensive metaphysical information about how we create our reality. I have been looking for something like this. I am so excited. At last I can figure out where my power is to make my life happier.* It was similar to the cult's idea of each person being responsible for what happened in their lives, but it did not promote worshipping a deity, an Ascended Master, or a religious figure. I was fascinated with learning about how our soul is both a perpetrator and a victim throughout many lifetimes and sometimes both within one lifetime. Unconsciously, I gained hope that I could access some kind of healing because I learned that as my awareness grew, I had a choice whether or not to play those roles.

On a fall day, I am driving in the station wagon with Steven in his car seat in the back. My mind wanders down an unexpected path. *I could kill myself right now just by letting go of the steering wheel. But I cannot do that. That would be bad for the baby. I am really miserable.* Finally, I am admitting the depth of my unhappiness to myself.

Three-year-old Steven is sitting on the potty. "If you go poop, you get some M and M's." I point to the special jar filled with colorful candies. "Let's look and see if you get any." Steven and I gaze together into the empty toilet.

"I'll do it on Monday," he tells me. My shoulders drop. *I feel like throwing the damn jar. Please, God, give me patience. I do not know if I can keep my cool much longer. I need help with parenting Steven. I feel so depressed about everything.*

I am overwhelmed with waves of powerlessness, depression and feeling trapped as a mother. *I know, I will go to graduate school.* I was groping for sanity. The structure of grad school gave me a false sense of control. Ed and I talk about having another child, and with my master's program underway, it seems like the perfect time. *This child is going to have to realize that I have a career and am not just a mom.*

I really want a girl. I really want a girl. I really want a girl to bring some kind of softness into my life. I find I am pregnant. "Just as I planned," I say.

"Let's play ET." I am seven months pregnant when four-year-old Steven makes his appeal.

"Ok," I respond, easing my belly down to the floor.

Steven's face lights up as he totters like ET to the imaginary refrigerator and tips his head back to drink beer after beer after beer, imitating his favorite scene from the movie. Suddenly Steven's animated body crumbles in a "drunken" pile on the floor, arms and legs wiggling with excitement. I reach over and tickle Steven's tummy. *It feels so good to laugh with Steven.*

"Again," he requests.

There are many iterations of this very scene, as many as I can abide. *It might be hard to find time for Steven once the new baby comes. Will I be able to handle two children?*

With my mind having decided that grad school would give me a boost in my life, I accept the challenge of commuting thirty miles away from home. I am dropping Steven off at the babysitter's home. When we pull up to her house, I feel Steven's kicks vibrating on the back of the passenger seat in protest. *Please do not make this hard on me. Don't you see, Steven, I have to do this?* I open the door of the car and insist that Steven come along. My mind is rationalizing so I do not feel his pain. *Don't worry. Steven will be fine once he gets inside. And most importantly, once I have a counseling degree, I will have a place in this world. I have got to do this. I have a right to get a degree and have prestige and a career. Everything is going to be fine.*

Nicholas arrived in 1982. *It is not a girl.* There was no joy on Ed's face. His first response was, "We're not going for number three just because this isn't a girl." Nicholas slept a lot and was easy to soothe. *He does not scream all the time. I cannot believe how well things are going.*

Through memory retrieval over several years, I have reclaimed what happened with my son, Nicholas, my sister, and her children not long after his birth.

It is spring 1983. An alter part of my personality has been trained and prepared to give away my son to a ritual ceremony. My thirty-two-year-old alter, whose presence I discovered many years later, was told it was time for Nicholas' dedication ceremony. *I do not know exactly where I am because someone picked us up in the night and drove us to this secluded spot outside of town. I am in a mental fog. I feel the chilly air on my face, and we are outside. I glance around and note that Dawn and her children and Steven are all present. They have told me, "Nicholas will be dedicated to a program for training in the Sciences so he can grow up and make a great contribution. Your family is part of the illumined ones who have a right to be leaders of our world. In due time, your children will be given high positions." Three ritual participants in robes stand side by side, and one reaches toward me with their silent demand for my child. I see dark, bony hands ready to clutch and claim my baby. I pull Nicholas closer to my heart, instinctively wanting to protect him from these people. Yet a force inside of me feels like I have no choice. I am also experiencing my tender emotions of not wanting to let go of my boy. I am nauseous and shaking and soon these sensations give way to the sounds of chanting. This reinforces my alter who is aligned with the agenda to follow through with the ceremony. I hear a crackling fire as they pass me a chalice from which I drink. The voice inside of my head saying "don't hurt my baby" starts to fade as the effects of the liquid begin to take me into a familiar, hazy world where rabbits squeal and time slows down. I disconnect from the sadness in my heart as the drug overtakes my senses, and a ritual alter takes over my person. I am no longer the loving mother I most identify with. I surrender Nicholas to my authorities, and, in this moment, our bond is violated.*

The most difficult part of all the memory retrieval work was realizing that in my split alters, I had been trained to give away and hurt my own children.

CHAPTER EIGHT

An Invitation from Nature

My pursuit in graduate school was fueled by my curiosity about why I was so depressed. *Is it because of my current family or my past family? I do not know.* I was curious about family dynamics too. *What makes a healthy family? I wonder why Steven is so angry. I certainly am not that angry. How can we change our family patterns?* My emotions had been thawing out more and more since Steven's birth. Although I consumed self-help books, desiring to understand myself and my life, I ended up using them to rationalize and did not get professional help. I kept myself in denial of my deeper pain, telling myself: *I have a lot of understanding about life. I do not think a counselor can tell me anything I do not already know. Plus, I just would not trust them.*

With my counseling degree completed in 1984, I half-heartedly looked for a job. My guilt about not contributing to the family finances was pinching me. *I still do not feel ready to help other people even though I have my master's now. How am I going to be able to make some money?* We were still squeaking by on Ed's salary, when an opportunity for work came along in 1986 that I felt I could handle. Ed's friend, Max, was the director of a program for gifted and talented children whose ages go up to tenth graders. "I would love to have you come and teach in our summer program, Beth." Steven had attended the program for a couple summers, so I was somewhat familiar with it. *It is not a counseling job, per se, but it is something new.* By May, in anticipation of my new job, my chest was heavy with bronchitis, and I carried a fearful knot in my gut. *I am so scared. What am I doing? I have never taught older kids before.* Maybe *this could be fun. But what if they do not like me? What if I do not like them? Thank goodness it is only part-time. I am sure I can make it through four weeks.*

After two weeks of teaching, I started feeling valued again, just like when I had started teaching in 1972. My sense of self expanded beyond motherhood.

In Spring of 1987, Max and his wife, Georgia, invited us to go on a backpacking adventure with them. "We're taking a group to the Grand Canyon during spring break," they announced. "Maybe you all would like to come."

"Hmmm," I said, beginning to consider the possibility. Excitement started to bubble up in my chest. "Sounds like fun. I'll talk it over with Ed and let you know."

"I think Nicholas is too young for a trip like that," Ed declared in a flat matter-of-fact tone. My moment of enthusiasm for a happy family adventure dissolved as I felt my hope give way to Ed's practical considerations. *Maybe he is right. For sure it will not work if we aren't both excited about it.* "Why don't you go with Steven and I'll stay home with Nicholas," Ed offered. I could not turn his offer down.

With Georgia and Max's encouragement, I decided to invite two of my siblings, Dawn and our younger brother, on the trip. *We have never done anything like this together. I think it could be fun.* I felt my spirit lifting, even while I was disappointed to leave Ed and Nicholas behind. My childhood family never took adventures in nature. Unconsciously I was programmed to be repulsed from nature because it meant rituals of terror performed in the darkness of night.

The sun was shining bright and warm as I stood on the hilltop waiting for Dawn to arrive. When I spotted her, my eyes widened with alarm, and my heart started racing. *Oh my god, what has happened to her? Is she going to be able to make the hike? Her face is pale and sagging.* The fear I felt was familiar. There were countless times in our day life when my adrenaline spiked, and I was very afraid for her safety even though I did not know details of what was happening to either one of us. I hugged her tightly and fell into our family habit of pretending not to see. *Do not say anything right now.*

One morning, we queued up to hike to Havasu falls. My feet felt sturdy on the hardened dirt along the trail. The earthy fragrance tickled my nose, and I flexed my knees as I bounced along the path in eager anticipation of the beauty I was about to see. Reaching the waterfall required us to negotiate a steep descent. "There will be steps carved into the rock and a rope to hang on to. Just take your time, and you will be fine," our hike leader advised. I found my courage and trusted my footing. I could hear the thundering power of the waterfall even before I could see it, and I felt it in the pores of my skin and the pulse of my blood. I was coming alive and so was Dawn. A lightness appeared on her face, and we were in awe over the magnificence before us.

On the third day, our dirty hair called our attention. Dawn bent over the wash bowl in the river, as I carefully poured water on her scalp. "Oh, Dawn. What is that?" I felt a large bump on her head.

"That bastard kept me up all night and hit my head against the wall." She spit her words out and her hidden anger now seethed in the space between us. Her husband was obviously haranguing my sister, trying to bully her into not coming. She had not talked about her abusive marriage or her deeper feelings before. *Why doesn't she leave him? I am worried for my nieces, too.* Just like I hid my depression, she hid her abusive marriage. Now, I was beginning to realize the extent of the violence she endured. It was a quiet triumph in our lives to have made it to the hilltop. We were opening to something we had not yet defined.

When I returned home, I wrote a poem to remind myself of my sensual experiences, my initiation into knowing life in more fullness. When the tedium of daily routines threatened to drown me, I had my poem to bring back loving memories to my flesh and soul.

Supai Song

Oh Earth, I knew your kiss as I rested on my pillow
Felt your gentle arms caress me as I slept.
Your rushing waters calmed my furor as I journeyed down
the pathway
Searching for the answers only dreams could tell.

I heard your heartbeat as I lay there in its rhythm soft and steady
Never once did you desert my weary soul.
You sent me fragrances of splendor, wrapped in honey
blossom petals
Kissed by sunlight in their early morning pose.

Plucked a plum, I did, from heaven as your nighttime sky
did twinkle
Lighting passageways I thought had long been closed
You sent my soul upon a journey to a place I had forgotten
Reminding me that what was once will always be.

You spoke your truth in just a whisper as we winded
through the canyon
Lead me to the cliff that I had feared so long.
Then wrote a message with a feather, flying free, oh free forever,
Gave me winged flight to soar, my Supai song.

April 12, 1987

I now had awareness that life indeed did have more to offer, and I longed for the company of other adults. Over the next three years, I reached out to connect with other people. I joined a public speaking club, fulfilling a desire I held to learn to speak and inspire others. Occasionally I travelled to regional meetings with the club, smiling as I hugged my husband and children good-bye for the day. And I returned to the summer program each year, eventually becoming an administrator.

My perspective about my life became more optimistic for myself but less positive about Ed. I watched Ed's lack of control over his anger. It is a Saturday morning and Nicholas and Steven are arguing. "I want to watch The Care Bears," Nicholas declares.

"No. They are so dumb. Care Bears are for babies. It's time for Teenage Mutant Ninja Turtles," Steven counters as he gets up to switch the television channel. "Don't be such a little baby." The argument intensifies.

Ed suddenly bursts into the room with a loud roar. I am stunned. His anger chokes the very breath out of me, and the room becomes silent. No one moves. *This is not good for the boys. Ed's anger is scary. Doesn't he know how damaging his behavior can be?* I cannot find the words to tell Ed that this is a problem. I am numb and mute. Sadness, frustration, shame, hopelessness, depression, and loneliness form a cocktail of emotions that swirl about me. I want relief, but I do not know where to find it.

I said *yes* again when Max and Georgia organized another trip to Supai in 1990, three years later. I could already smell the fresh air and feel the "good tired" in my legs. *Nicholas is old enough now to handle this adventure. But can we do it as a family? Will Ed be willing? He never wants to go anywhere or do anything. I cannot even get him to do date night, so I doubt it. He has become so boring.*

Ed was no more ready to go backpacking this time than he had been the first time. My clenched jaw held back my anger as I resigned myself to what was. In that moment, I stuffed down the questions that I was going to have to eventually face about my marriage. "Ed, I need to take some time away for myself. Steven only complains about camping so I would like to leave him home. Would you be willing to take care of the kids while I go?" I felt a little guilty about leaving Ed with the kids, but I justified my decision. *It is Ed's fault. If he were not so resistant, things would be better.*

I took a deep breath that spread through my whole body as the burnt orange canyon walls greeted me. My backpack weighed firmly on my shoulders, and I began my descent, following the switchbacks down into the canyon. *I need comfort, space, time to form my questions.* For the next few days, I was like an embryo resting in the canyon's womb unaware of what my life might be after I emerged.

I confided in Georgia. She accepted my tales of woe without giving me unwanted advice. "Do you think you'll stay with Ed?" she gently asked.

"Yeah, I guess we'll just live parallel lives under the same roof yet go our separate ways," I concluded. "We are already doing that pretty much anyway."

I had come alive once again in the surroundings of Supai. What a contrast this was to the robotic life I led with Ed. An inner desire for change was ever present. I wanted more from life. I wanted more from Ed. I wondered what was going to happen in my marriage now that I could no longer tolerate my life in its current state. Ed and I had our obligatory routines but little more. *I do not think Ed is going to change.* My heart was heavy with the hopelessness of my marriage.

CHAPTER NINE

For Better or Worse:
Divorce

It is the fourth day since I have been home from Supai. My feelings are squelched and churning as I try to figure out my course of action. The pressure of my bottled-up feelings has been building each day that I have been home. I walk into the living room where Ed is relaxing. "I need to talk with you, Ed." He looks at me, a frown of puzzlement knitting his eyebrows together.

"I'm not happy." I begin to peel away the first layer of truth. "We don't do things together. What kind of family are we?" I continue to pour my world of hurt and disappointment out into the space between us. "I was hoping that the second trip to Supai would happen so I could believe that you wanted to be together as a family. You keep telling the kids that you will take them camping and here was the perfect opportunity, but you declined. You are unhappy with your job. You get angry with the kids all the time. Is there anything that makes you happy? I don't know how much longer I can do this."

Ed throws me a glance, then stares off to the side of me. He looks numb and pale. I want to cry but I am cold and detached. I wish I could shake a response out of him, but he remains still, stunned. I feel weak and tired and have nothing else to say.

For the next few days, I keep the discussion going in my head. *Ed's not a bad person but I do not think we want the same things in life. He is a good provider, but he does not want to take any risks. He does not want to grow. I know he loves his kids, but he does not even realize how he affects them. He does not cheat on me or hit me; he just feels like he is dead. Steven is so negative, just like his father. I am afraid that when he becomes a teenager, he will kill himself if I do not make changes. It is terrible for the kids to be around two people who do not love each other. I cannot live without hope of change. We will all be better off if Ed and I divorce. I am afraid I will never feel close to Ed again. This mental debate is driving me crazy. That is it. I am going to divorce him.*

Three days later, Ed responds to me. By this time, it is too late. I have no interest in hearing him. And I am angry that it has taken him so long to respond. I realize now, many years later, that I used my education to rationalize divorce instead of figuring out how to heal.

"Don't I get a say in all this? I don't want to be a divorced man and not be able to see my children every day," Ed says with tears in his eyes. I steel my heart to his sadness. *It is too late now. I am not responsible for Ed's feelings. I cannot have empathy or sympathy for Ed. I have to look after my own feelings.* I did not consider that Ed could grow if we sought help with our communication. I was making my misery all about him. *Surely things will improve once I divorce Ed.*

"We need to tell the children together," Ed says. I agree.

A couple days later, I am getting ready to take the boys on an errand with me. Steven and Nicholas are waiting in the car. I slam the door after I get in. All the tension in my body makes me want to scream but I do not. I let out a deep sigh. My ability to pretend that everything is fine has escaped me. "What's wrong, Mom?" Steven asks. "Is it about Dad? Are you guys going to get a divorce?"

My guilt comes crashing down and my face is flushing hot. I feel trapped. "Yes," I say.

"But you told us you guys would never get a divorce," Nicholas says. "You promised." His voice is full of disbelief. I feel my butt tighten, my arms flinch, my neck tense. My guilt travels inward into my muscles as they stiffen.

"I'm sorry," I say tersely. "Your dad and I just can't work things out." I exhale with exasperation. *Well shit, I did not wait for Ed.*

It is the end of summer in 1990. Our divorce will be official in the fall. Steven is turning twelve and Nicholas will be eight in a couple of months. I like our small apartment whose number happens to be my lucky number, 1111. Steven has his own room. Nicholas has the sunroom for his bedroom. Every night, I meld with my bed, surrounded by my essentials, a desk, and a dresser. Cozy. *I feel held in this small space.* I now stand at the sink looking at my reflection in the mirror. *So, this is what a divorced woman looks like.* The lines around my eyes have deepened. There is a distinct downward sag around my mouth. *I am on my own now. Ed is thirty miles away.* I look directly into my hazel green eyes. *It is Max's idea for me to come here and get a doctoral degree. Why not? I cannot think of any other direction to go. I can do this. I am determined.*

It is a week before the semester starts at the university. My neck muscles are rocks sitting on my shoulders. Slight nausea sits in the pit of my stomach. *I must go in today, even though the boys do not start school for another ten days. My kids need me here in this new city. I wish I could just hang out with them. But I need to go to work, create my study schedule, keep the household running and be a Mom. How am I ever going to do it all?* I exhale deeply, overwhelm washing over me and leaving a knot in my throat. I give the boys a kiss and go out the door.

A couple months later, it is bedtime at the end of a school day. I am sitting at the edge of Nicholas' bed, tucking him in and rubbing his back. "Mom," Nicholas says. His voice is quivering. "Are you going to leave me?"

I am dumbfounded. My heart skips a beat. "Where on earth did you get that idea?"

"Well, you left Dad." I am suddenly aware of Nicholas' small, slender frame. He looks so vulnerable.

"Oh my gosh, Nicholas, no! I would rather cut off my arm than leave you. I love you!" I gather him up into my arms. *I love you so much.* As I am holding my son, I am shocked by his perceptions, and now that I am aware, I am shocked that I did not consider how my children might be feeling. At this time in my life, I had to have tunnel vision, believing this was for the best for all. I could not consider any feelings or thoughts that would suggest differently, or I would have crumbled.

Our first Christmas after the divorce we head to my brother's home in California, with big plans to go to Disneyland. *I want them to have a good Christmas, something special to help them adjust to our new life.* Steven is twelve; Nicholas is eight. We are sitting in the car waiting for my brother to run an errand when Steven asks with disgust, "Why is this taking so long?" He is moaning and complaining angrily. *Oh no. Here we go again. He grouched around all morning. He is being such a brat.*

"It'll just be a few minutes. Please be patient," I plead.

"This trip is just as boring as I thought it would be," Steven adds. "I hate this trip."

My rage moves from zero to ten, and my hand flies across Steven's face. "Stop being so negative about everything. I can't stand to be around you when you are that way." *Holy shit. I just hit my kid.* I sit in silence, stunned with my behavior. *At least he has shut up.* I calm down and guilt sets in immediately. *I am so tired of hearing his complaints. But I do not want to hit my kids. What kind of horrible mother am I?* "Steven, I'm sorry I slapped you. That was not right, but I really could not take your attitude for another minute. I just lost it with you." My shoulders sag as I lie back against the headrest.

I have started to realize that I can no longer blame Ed. He is not the cause of my unhappiness. Now that I do not have to consider Ed's needs on a daily basis, I have space to experience myself, and the rage that was always under the surface is showing itself. My life does not feel better. I am waking up to deeper layers of what has always been inside.

I cannot wait to crawl into bed each evening to escape into sleep. As I close my eyes, I feel like I am swinging untethered in a sea of anxiety with nothing to ground me. I do not know where to find relief. I meditate and pray. What is the loving thing to do? The answer that comes surprises me. It is to get on an anti-depressant. But I do not believe in taking anti-depressants. Nonetheless, I do. Without therapy, I have no other coping mechanisms to rely on.

CHAPTER TEN

A Crack in my Denial

I t is 1994. The boys, ages eleven and fifteen, and I eagerly
anticipate getting out of town to go visit Aunt Dawn
during spring break. They are looking forward to seeing
their cousins.

Steven and Nicholas bound into Dawn's house with a
surge of energy. Endless hours would pass as they played the
desirable games that only older, adored cousins can offer.

We are not long into the visit. I realize that Dawn, me,
my other sister, and our mother all divorced after seventeen
and a half years of marriage. How odd. What is that about?
With all these questions in my mind, Dawn invites me to
sit down with her in the family room. "I have something to
tell you," she says. Her voice has an edge of defense. Her
words are terse with a righteous, almost preachy tone. Her
face is tight. Her words hit me like a fist in the stomach.
Half conscious, barely breathing, I hear: "Father's penis…
raped me… dead rabbits… red… black… urine… semen…
Satanic Ritual Abuse…"

My first inner reaction is *DANGER! DANGER! DANGER!* *Impossible.* I am tumbling down a dark hole and going numb. *Oh my god!* I hold my breath. In this moment, hearing Dawn's words that are vibrating her truth, I cannot move, yet deep inside I feel a tremble moving upward from my gut, beginning to shake loose the foundation of my denial. We stare at each other in silence. Finally, I am ready to speak.

"Dawn, why didn't you tell me earlier?"

Dawn's face constricts in pain. "Every time I tried to tell you about Mom, you just blamed me, Beth. You made it all my fault because I was so angry. You've always defended Mom." She is staring at me. Her eyes are penetrating mine with the harsh glare of betrayal.

She continues. "Mom only cares about superficial stuff like what's on the menu at restaurants. She and Dad live in this pretend world of trying to impress other people. With all their money, they wouldn't even loan me the three thousand dollars I desperately needed for the lawyer when I was trying to leave my abusive marriage." Her voice dripped with contempt.

A deep shiver travels up my spine, and quiet fills the room. Her words have created a chasm in me where truth is erupting beyond my control. "Dawn, I'm so sorry. I just didn't know."

That night as I tried to sleep, I tossed and turned and slept fitfully. My arms and legs pulled inward as I hugged myself like a baby, trying to stop the shaking sensations that wracked my body. My terror was erupting beyond my control. When I awoke in the morning, before words formed, I was thick with a deep sense of dread. Laying there in bed, staring at the ceiling, a small ray of light penetrated my consciousness. *This could be the reason why I have hated my life, felt such misery, and have been so depressed. We have been part of something more frightening than I can put into words.* A slow, long sigh escaped my lips as a compassionate wave of understanding washed over me. I crossed my arms and embraced my shoulders, rocking myself back and forth. *Although I am ashamed that I have been in such denial, there is also a ray of hope that I may be able to move forward. Somehow, I do not know how, somehow, I will keep moving forward.*

I was not who I thought I was. I had lived for over forty years without awareness of many aspects of my life. *I cannot push this river to try and remember, but I want to know everything, even though I am terrified of what I will discover.*

Having opened to Dawn's communication, she and I now are allies. After several weeks of phone talks, she says, "I have a book to recommend, Beth." I go and purchase the large paperback, *Safe Passage to Healing, A Guide for Survivors of Ritual Abuse* (Oksana, 1994). My sister validates my discoveries. She says, "You'll see that there are many others who have uncovered memories of SRA. It is real. It is not made up."

I read with great curiosity, beginning to consider the depth of horror that SRA encompasses. *Who hurt me? Was it my father? My mother? How am I going to figure out the truth? How can humans be this cruel? It is hard to believe that this has happened to me. How am I going to access what happened to me?* I read that other survivors try self-hypnosis. So, I try self-hypnosis. I keep seeing an eye. Nothing makes sense. I am blocked. I feel nothing but frustration. *I am going to need help to get to my memories. Where can I find help?*

My mind goes into high gear, scanning my conscious memory for childhood clues. I have no conscious memories of going to a ritual, being tortured, or killing animals. I flash to the story that my mother has told me over and over since I was five. "You used to hold your breath until you passed out." I sink into my body to feel this memory. I can recall the feeling of walking home from the neighbor's house. I could not feel my mother's presence. It is as if I am holding the hand of a manikin. "Tighter, Mommy, tighter," I would plead. I want her to grip my hand so I can really feel her there. I beg once again, "Tighter." I am desperate for this connection. *I cannot feel Mommy.* A wave of heat rises in my belly and constricts my chest. I grit my teeth and hold my breath, crumbling to the cement. The next thing I know, my mother is holding me up. *Ah, there she is.* As a sixty-eight-year old woman, writing about this story, I see I was desperate for connection. I had no anchor for safety. I wanted to die, even at five.

My understanding of myself increased as I read Oksana's book. I was struck by something she said about children who write backwards. She reported this characteristic in some ritual survivors. Around the age of eight, I liked to write backwards and became very good at it. This was such an unusual clue and a concrete example that clearly applied to me. It helped validate that I had been programmed during rituals.

For the next three months, the daily routines of my life were a welcome distraction that kept me going despite the continual sense of trepidation that I carried. It is a typical morning, I go to check on Nicholas. There he is, standing by the sink, toothbrush suspended in mid-air as he stares ahead. I am looking at him with new eyes. He is entranced in thought, almost floating. I drive him to school, and as we stop at the curb, he makes no move to get out of the car. "Are you going to be able to go in?" I ask. I start to feel deep sadness for him and am afraid of what I do not know. "If you need to stay home, I'll let you." *We usually do not have that option, but today it feels important to not push him.* We drive back home together. I had always told myself that Nicholas was just a highly imaginative, gifted kid, but now I know something horrible has happened to me that I have denied. How has that affected my children, my husband, Dawn and me, and all my significant relationships? I feel desperate to find the truth so that I can help my children heal as well. *Oh, my goodness. Nicholas is not healthy.*

FINDING A THERAPIST OR TWO OR THREE OR FOUR...

My research tells me that ritual survivors can be programmed to be highly functional. That was me. That made it even harder for me to admit that I needed help. It is 1995 when I finally decide to go to therapy. I had reached a threshold in my mental understanding along with all the synchronicities of Dawn's sharing, and I am finally ready to get help.

It was a beautiful, sunny day as I entered the therapist's office. After the preliminaries, she asked, "What brings you here, Beth?"

"I think that I was sexually violated as a child, and yet I don't have mental recall of anything, you know. Being in the counseling field myself, I know about repressed memories." I watch myself not mentioning SRA. *I am not ready to speak of that out loud. My mind goes back and forth between believing and not believing.* "I think maybe I'm just making this whole thing up," I offer.

"Yes, that is a common thought. Would you like to explore your body sensations and see where that leads us?" she suggests. "I can regress you and see what we find out."

"Well, I also believe that I am responsible for my life and that I somehow created this," I add. *I doubt that she believes in the spiritual principles about creating one's own reality like I do. I do not know if I will be able to work with her.*

"Well, if you are saying that you are at fault for your childhood abuse, I completely disagree," she says. "Is that what you mean?"

"No, not exactly." *I like her well enough. I will just drop the spiritual discussion and see what help I can get from her. I need to start somewhere.*

I close my eyes and relax. "I feel strange, like I am paralyzed, well not exactly, it's hard to describe. The sensation is that of being hard and metal-like." *I have experienced these sensations many times when lying in bed at night.*

"Are you in something that is hard and metal?" she asks.

"No. My body is like that." My body feels as if it is configured like a box with square corners. "I also feel tingling in my genitals."

"The tingling may be a memory of sexual stimulation," she informs me.

Oh. This is interesting. This must be what a body memory is.

FATHER'S LETTER

A few weeks later, I was so glad to have a therapist so I could discuss a letter I had just received. "I got a letter from my biological father this week. I am sorry I ever reached out to him. I don't want to stay in contact." I was confused and angry. When a friend of his had tracked me down, I agreed to be in touch with him. I was now forty-four years old, and I had an idea that I should heal my relationship with him.

"Tell me what has come up for you with the letter." She is looking at me with an open, steady gaze. *She really wants to know. That is so cool. Someone is listening.*

"He thinks he's a wise, spiritual soul. Listen to this part of his letter: 'I know you quite well. You are here [in this lifetime] because I agreed to give you the opportunity. In fact, it takes four persons (sic) agreement before anyone is born. Since these decisions are made at the inner level, they aren't easily remembered by everyone, but the prospective father, mother, the soul who wants to come, and the Holy Spirit must all agree, even in cases of incest." I look up at her but gaze past her, directing hatred at my invisible father. My leg is twitching with the desire to give him a swift kick.

"Has he ever acknowledged the incest he perpetrated?"

"No. Are you kidding? He paints himself as a spiritual know-it-all." *He is trying to justify his incest with spiritual principles without taking any ownership for the violation.* "Then later in the letter he is trying to guilt me for backing away from him, saying that I am not following my heart and only want the approval of others." My skin is crawling with disgust. His words feel like energetic tentacles that want to wrap themselves around me. I take a deeper breath to ward off the feeling of constriction in my lungs. *He is so manipulative.*

"Just breathe, Beth. These are powerful feelings that are coming forward for you. Allow yourself to be with them."

"I know I have unfinished business with him, but in light of his distorted thinking, I cannot imagine him being able to hear any viewpoint other than his own." My body feels tight and a familiar feeling of being trapped settles into my bones.

"You have plenty of time to sort this out. There is no need to do anything or take any action unless it feels right to you." I exhale deeply into that empowering idea.

At the end of his letter, he invites me to come to an eleven-day conference conducted by Elizabeth Clare Prophet of *The Summit Lighthouse*, saying he would pay up to one thousand dollars to make it possible for me to come. *Are you kidding me? I would not take one step down that slippery slope of spiritual brainwashing, lies and manipulation. No thank you. I have a boundary. Yay!*

CONFRONTING MOM

During this era of therapy sessions, my mother had learned from Dawn her memories of ritual abuse. Mom has now flown in for a visit with me. It is not long before she brings up the information Dawn has shared with her. We are sitting catty corner to one another at my dining table, her body pulled inward toward herself. "I have no memory of what Dawn is talking about." These are the first words she speaks. My mother's voice is monotone and flat, without concern or caring. She seems to only be interested in making her disclaimer.

I had a secret hope that she, too, would consider that she was disassociated and would take time for self-reflection. *Does not remembering mean she did not participate? Look at me. Look at Dawn.* I look at her, waiting for some emotion of sadness or horror. Nothing. Only flat affect and absent response. I could not detect even a tiny part of her that wanted to know what had happened. *How did Mom get this way? How could she be so void of emotion?* And the answer comes. *This is my lineage. This is how I have been. My mother is numb. I am numb. How many generations back does this go in my family?* I am shocked as I accept that this is my family heritage.

As I read about trauma, I see that numbness is a typical symptom, living life as a robot. My mind continues to go back and forth arguing with itself. *I see this could really be true, but nothing that bad could have happened to me without conscious memory. My therapist keeps guiding me into my feelings, but I am not sure I trust that process. I trust my intellect more than my body.* I take a break from therapy. *I just want to have a regular life for a while and pretend none of this ever happened.*

After months of plodding along, I hear of a therapist who works with SRA clients. *Damn. It is time to dive in again.* This next therapist has a lot of information about SRA, validating my symptoms, and using regression therapy. I start to feel the despair in my body and soul. I am finally accepting that I have not been just sexually abused. I am a child of SRA. I now understand that my body is the place that memories are stored, so I also seek out body work to unlock more of what my body knows.

I am on the massage table with Ulli. Her touch is soft, as she runs her hands down my legs in a welcoming greeting. Her voice is firm and clear when she asks me to tell her what

I think my body needs. *I want to feel good. No pain, please.* After several sessions, I am convinced that her fingers are magical in their ability to read my body. She gives me some feedback. "There is a barrier in your muscle tissue that you have erected to keep the information in your lower body from your awareness. It's like you have an army protecting you from your own knowing." I can feel the wall of division between my upper body and lower body. *It makes sense why I do not have memory.* I eventually stop with this therapist and my life becomes a walking prayer.

Dear God, I know that something happened, and I need to understand myself and my life. I cannot be whole until I do. Please show me the way. It has become more and more clear that my healing cannot be separate from my spiritual journey. All my therapists, so far, do not understand that my healing is my path of evolution for my soul. God, I do not know when, where, or how, but I trust You hear me and will guide me to the right person and circumstance to unlock what I cannot know needs to be unlocked. There is purpose for my life. Help me to understand what that is.

"Hello Dawn. It is me. It is so nice to have you to talk to. I cannot imagine going through this without you. So many people do not have anyone, especially not a family member. Steven has been living with Ed and has just graduated college. I think he has channeled all his anger into flying airplanes. Now that Nicholas is living near you, I rarely hear from him. I feel scared; I hope he does not go back to cutting himself. The counseling he got is just the beginning of uncovering what is going on with him. How much do you think our kids have been hurt? Now that I have an empty nest, I do not think I can hold on much longer here at the university. I've been thinking of leaving this area."

"Why don't you move back here?" Dawn asks. I knew I needed to find a new location, but I had not seriously considered returning home until that moment. It was now obvious.

In 2001, I move back to the city where I was born where much of the trauma had occurred. Dawn and I can now support one another to heal.

CHAPTER ELEVEN

A Date with Destiny

I am in my new home which is on the same street that Dawn lives on. I have just returned from substitute teaching on a beautiful March afternoon. I press the red blinking light on my answering machine.

"Hello Beth. I am having a gathering at my house tonight." It is Angie, whom I have recently met at a spiritual conference. "A friend of mine, Robin, who does breathwork is leading the group. Call me if you want to come." *Interesting that she thought to invite me.*

I call and she puts Robin on the phone. As I talk with Robin, I feel something inside of me pulled to go to the group. *But I hate groups. I do not want to do that.* I say to Angie, "I'll be there." *Oh God, what did I just commit to? Breathwork?*

I am at Angie's house, and Robin welcomes everyone, asking us to form a circle. Her smile fills the entire room. She starts to share her beliefs. "Healing is about learning to love *everything.*"

How the hell am I supposed to love torture? I have always known that love is the great healing force in the universe. How is this going to work? Robin continues to share her personal story with conviction because her processes come from healing herself. She seems to be very open and transparent, not like other therapists. She calls herself a spiritual healer and facilitator.

Robin explains, "Our body holds denied experiences; and when we can express through our physical and emotional sensations and receive them consciously, our being and inner children experience this as love. We are giving freedom to what has been denied and receiving our body's experience without judging it. Breathwork is a tool to awaken our denied experiences and body memories and to invite our life force and spirit to heal us."

After a short introduction, she instructs our group of five or six to lie down on the floor. "Breathe through your mouth using big, deep, fast breaths. Send your breath down to your belly," she advises. My breathing increases in depth and frequency. *My mouth is so dry. This feels so strange. I do not know how long I can keep this going.* My hands tingle. The space behind my eyes becomes fiery white. Nothing exists for a split second. When I come back to awareness, I continue to breathe but now it is easier.

She continues to guide us, "Use your voice. Express whatever wants to come out."

"Eeeeeeeeee, aaaaaaaaaaah." I am screaming, shrieking. Heat is moving up my lower body and my torso. I am kicking. I am shaking. My legs are moving spontaneously. I want to run. I feel a warm hand touching my shoulder. I open my eyes, and Robin grasps my hands, looking directly into my eyes. *I feel seen. She can feel and see my pain.* Her compassionate gaze reaches deep into my soul. I feel a connection to her that I have never experienced with any other facilitator. She invites me back to my breath, and now my body is shaking all over. My tense, frozen muscles are defrosting, yet strangely, I feel safe and contained. Robin guides me to slow my breath and come back to present time. I hug myself and squeeze my arms, affirming self-loving words with self touch. We all sit up.

Robin suggests we look into each other's eyes, orienting us into connection with each other in present time. *Wow. I feel more connected to myself.* Robin reminds the group to reach out for help if any flashbacks of memories come up or if we have any questions about our experience. I commit to a six-week series with the group.

Five weeks later, I am in the group and a voice inside is ranting. *I hate myself. I hate these awful feelings. I wish I were as far along as Carolyn is. I am not as good as Carolyn.* I am judging my process in the midst of trying to heal.

Robin asks, "How was the session for you tonight, Beth?"

My lips are pressed tight. *I do not want to talk. I feel ashamed.* I finally respond, "I felt very uncomfortable. I feel I'm not as good as everyone else in the group."

Her eyes meet mine. "You are starting to feel what is in your body," she says. "The breath is what moves the hatred out of the cells. This is a good sign that you are feeling your hatred."

"Hatred? Oh, yeah, I guess I am hating myself." I was beginning to understand that loving my feelings meant feeling them. I was a master at avoiding my feelings. *Why do I have to feel so shitty in order to heal?* Yet, Robin's presence, processes and words made sense to me. She had a unique combination of talents: a trust in the healing process of love, psychic gifts, and two master's degrees that had trained her as a facilitator. I began to trust myself and see that my spiritual guidance had led me to Robin for the deep healing work that I had prayed for during the last decade.

After the group, I continue to reach out to Robin for individual session work. For the next few months, I work with Robin and her husband. "We are healing the eternal soul," she states, "not just sexual trauma." *Yes, this is what I want!* All sessions are recorded so I can go back and review the information and use the tools I am learning to continue to go deeper within myself. I also learn that I have splintered into various parts, fragments. These parts have "helpers" attached. Some people would call these helpers dark spirits. Robin calls them entities that are shrouding my true self. These entities come not only to assist in satanic rituals but to serve the amnesia so I cannot feel or remember what has happened to me.

She continues to explain. "Healing your self-hatred means going deeply into your body memory. To really engage at this deep level, you need to have plenty of time and space for yourself. For deeper work, I offer an experience, an Intensive. Are you interested?"

"Yes." My voice is clear and firm. I am to set aside six consecutive days where she, her husband Joseph, and another facilitator will assist me. I am ready for this huge step in my life.

CHAPTER TWELVE

My First Intensive

I t is Fall 2003. Robin has prepared me for my Intensive. "You will need to have a helper available each evening to cook dinner for you and spend the night. It is important to have no responsibilities during this time and not be alone. After we remove the entities, you will have access to your body's memories. You don't want to be alone when the entities that have been protecting you have been removed and memories are coming."

Oh my god. What is going to happen? Am I going to completely fall apart? Will I become a blithering idiot, stuck in terror and unable to even get myself to the bathroom? My mind raced with worry.

I welcome Robin into my home. We embrace. She is driving one hundred twenty miles a day to be with me. The other practitioners will join her at specific times. I feel so grateful for her willingness and commitment to help me heal.

After doing sessions over the last several months, I now feel a deep connection and trust with Robin and Joseph. I am eager to find out more about my journey. I did not know it at the time, but we were on the precipice of discovering how to work with my deep despair, hopelessness, and terror. A template was being forged to show us how to work with my fragmented and divergent parts. This template was birthed out of the love frequency of Robin, Joseph, and me. My deep intention to heal was calling it forth. They were learning along with me because they had never had a client like me before.

There were many sessions and experiences during the six days of the Intensive. Hands-on energy work, breathwork, sounding, cathartic expression, role playing, inner sanctuary work and conscious soul retrieval were part of most sessions. Art therapy and dance/movement were also included.

I have chosen a foundational session from my Intensive to share with the reader. As I read the transcript from 2003, I am aware of how radically different this approach is to traditional forms of psychotherapy. It is a spiritual process. The strength of my desire to heal is what catalyzed Robin, Joseph, and the unseen helpers to assist me. I see, now, the power of the synergy, trust, and spiritual connection that Robin and Joseph had to their own self-love and Source and how that synergy helped me access my self-love.

The procedures that are detailed in the transcript emerged in the moment through prayer. We are constantly invoking my right to self-love. There was no predetermined protocol, only their willingness to be guided by their own inner spiritual selves. As they started reading my energy field, and I was giving them feedback, the language was called forth from the spirit of love to guide the healing. We took this journey together, a journey of love and trust.

The procedures of healing demonstrate the use of energy medicine through invocation and prayers, asking for spiritual help and support beyond the physical plane. These energies must be invoked because satanic rituals enroll

beings beyond the three-dimensional physical plane and use spiritual manipulation to entrap one's soul and identity. Satanic Ritual Abuse (SRA) is a manipulation of the human psyche. It is the manipulation of everything we call human through torture, using spiritual entities and beings to entrap the soul and psyche. The origins of SRA are not human; they come from other planes of existence. That is why there has been little success with mind therapy. Using the human impulse for safety, bonding, and connection, they manipulate our instinct to survive. Thus, the antidote must meet these energies where they reside, which is in the other planes of existence. We had to call on all the spiritual forces of love, healing, and good to make it safe for me to go into the dark.

The following is a direct transcription from my recording of the breakthrough session with Robin and Joseph. This is the core of my healing process. This is where I initially grounded and empowered my capacity to love the darkest of the dark in my soul. I can still feel the potency and power of the invocations, prayers, and processes that I experienced which laid the foundation for all further work.

I have used subheadings to help illuminate what is happening in each section. Much of the process involved using my voice to invoke my own emotional and spiritual will to command the right to heal these tortured parts. Robin leads me in dialog with aspects of myself that I have not consciously addressed ever before. Therefore, much of the transcript is me repeating loving communication to my parts. She is modeling how to lovingly connect and address the fractured parts that I have not been able to heal. A lot of the information that Robin reveals is coming directly from reading my soul and the field around me psychically. When Robin uses the term Christ, she is talking about Christ consciousness which is not the same as Jesus. (Please consult the Glossary for terms used that are specific to Robin's processes.)

Note to the Reader: Each reader will have their own experience with the transcript. For some, reading this material may create spontaneous healings because there is a specific way that the prayers and language were put together that can potentially activate an opening for healing. The language of the prayers is specific to healing SRA issues. It might also have the effect of triggering memory, and it may create, in some readers, heightened defenses. I invite you to notice your reactions and responses to reading this material.

SETTING THE SACRED SPACE WITH PRAYER

[Robin and Joseph have their eyes closed and they are tuning into the energies. We are all holding hands.]

Robin: Mother/Father God, All That Is, we open our sacred circle for the truth, love and power of Beth's Soul to integrate, and we now ask for the grace and the willingness to heal the body and surrender all separation in the soul and the heart and the mind and the emotions; and we call forth now all aspects of beingness that are ready to come into love or that don't even know that they are love. We ask now that that which has been held in the shadows reunite with the heart, the Christ, and we ask for the helpers from the Ascended Master realms and beyond. We call forth the angels that are helping Beth and Joseph and me. We ask Gaia to be present as we guide through the dimensionality of these patterns. [Gaia is a part of Robin that can see the eternal soul through all dimensions and looks for the cause in our consciousness for what is happening in

90

current time. Robin is still present in her personality while she accesses Gaia.] We bless now all the angels that are assisting and the guides and the guardians, and we ask you to make yourself known as we release your purposes into love.

Robin: The actual satanic overlay is up, with all that drawing work. [The previous day I had done some art therapy with Robin.] I am seeing the Satanic images. The drawings that you did yesterday are in your field. I can see the pictures, costumes and even beings that believe they are Satan. I sense parts of your soul that believe it is evil. I sense that this is where some of the rage is coming from, the part of you that believes it is Satan and evil and unlovable. It is living in the fear matrix. It is the hardest part of yourself to claim back and heal. Can you feel the emotional energy it holds? Where is it in your body? [She guides me to keep breathing.] May I put my hand on your belly?

WORKING WITH THE PART THAT DOES NOT WANT TO HEAL

The session continues.

Beth: Yes. [With Robin's hand on my belly, I continue to breathe.] I feel some nausea.

Robin: I sense there is a stabbing in the uterus, pain in the uterus and second chakra, that you may be able to go into. As long as you continue to breathe, it will move through your body very quickly. You do not have to stay in suffering, but we do have to call it back in, what has been denied.

Beth: Okay.

Robin: [Robin psychically hears a voice in my soul that she begins to make conscious. She expresses what she hears.] 'You can't heal me, you Mother Fucker. You cannot bring me into the light. My will is so strong. I can deny love.'

[I felt an intensifying pressure in my gut, my arms, and the heat of rage in my chest.]

Robin: Beth, we need to dialog with this part so you can feel it within yourself, and then we can work with it consciously. Can you hear what it is saying or believing?

Beth: I can just feel my own fear coming up about not being able to get beyond this. It is saying, 'Will this ever end? I will never get it. I'm unlovable.'

Robin: Yeah. That is really authentic, Beth. So just bless that part and say, 'I know that my belief is that I can't heal, that I'm so fragmented that I can't heal, and that's part of the lie, too, that they want me to believe, that fear is greater than love, that separation is greater than the love and unity. That's the game.' Just tell yourself, 'that's the game. It is just a game, and it is a game we played, and got played upon us. And as long as we believe that, then we are powerful enough to create that experience, but it is not the truth, the ultimate truth of Oneness and resurrection and transmutation.' [Robin begins to powerfully move her body, voice, and energy. She guides me into a dialog with my fear and resistance part.] Tell this part of the soul and personality, 'no part of me will be cast out. I have enough love with God to love it all.' You see, it wants to be cast out so it can still impact on your field on the unconscious realm.

92

I repeat what Robin coaches me to say.

Robin: [Robin begins to pray with Joseph.] I open with Joseph as a clear and perfect channel of divine truth of the Christ consciousness, and we ask now to serve Beth's intention to unify all aspects of soul, through love.

Beth: I intend to unify all aspects of soul with love. [This was my main intention which guided our work from then on.]

Robin: [In a very gentle voice] Is there a fear, Beth, if you see parts of yourself that have been violent that you will not be able to love them? What is the fear?

Beth: Yeah, probably that, and there are so many conscious parts of me that are out of touch with the violence. They just do not understand. I am confused.

Robin: That they have been separated for so long?

Beth: Yeah, I do not know if it is a mind thing. It is just fearful of seeing how this part could be so horrible. It would be difficult to look at it. It is the parts that have disidentified with it [the violent part].

Robin: Is there any fear that once you acknowledge and bring these aspects forth that it will take over and you will become that?

Beth: Probably. [I breathe deeply and feel into my fear.] Yeah.

Robin: What activates these parts more than anything?

Beth: Probably sexual experiences.

Robin: The love frequency does, as it is felt inside of you in your body. Sexuality is part of that. And so, you have stayed safe by avoiding the love frequency and sexual intimacy in your body. Do you see that?

Beth: Yeah. Yeah.

HOW DENIAL SERVES THE SATANIC

I had not been aware of how satanic energies worked through me until this session. Growing up, I had been taught in my day life that there was no such thing as a devil. As I read about satanic ritual abuse, I realized that there is a dark force that can be energized by turning away from love. My disbelief in these energies had been programmed in me so they would remain hidden from my conscious self. As I became aware of Robin's ability to see and hear the dark energies, I began moving out of denial. Once I shed the denial, my fear of being unable to heal could show itself. It had to be confronted, as well as my reluctance to look at my violent part. Even today, it is shocking to me to realize how the satanic energies were working through me.

INVITING CHRIST CONSCIOUSNESS AS THE HEALING POWER

The session continues.

Robin: [Robin looks at Joseph and notices a shift in his vibration and demeanor. Then she looks at me.] Can you feel or see the shift in Joseph?

Beth: [I look at Joseph. I feel a loving energy coming from him, especially emanating from his face.] Is it the love frequency? His Christ consciousness? [We begin to laugh. This bit of levity is welcome!]

Robin: Yeah, his Christ consciousness has been activated through the love frequency to help you heal. To stay safe, you have had to avoid the love frequency. I just want to honor that choice.

Robin: [Robin asks me to consider saying the following intention for self-compassion.] 'I honor the choice I made to keep myself from acting out and seeing these scary parts. I have avoided the love frequency as best I could. But now I know that it is through the love frequency, the Christ consciousness, that I can be healed. I can be reborn and retrieved.'

I repeat what Robin coaches me to say.

Robin: So, as you are looking at Joseph, looking as deeply into his eyes as you can, this is really going to activate you now, just through connecting to Joseph. Do you give him permission to activate your Christ consciousness?

Beth: I do.

Robin: Can you put that into words?

Beth: Joseph, I give you permission to activate my Christ consciousness.

Robin: Just breathe that in. Feel your body.

[I breathe in the experience of bringing love into my body. A subtle wave of relaxation descends downward into my limbs.]

TRANSFORMING THE CONSCIOUSNESS THAT DENIES LOVE

The following section describes merging with the beliefs in my body to awaken the vibrational holding, where they are held in my body, in my soul, and subconscious mind, so that when I release them, they go through my body and all levels of my being.

The session continues.

Robin: So, we need to discreate an agreement you made and that will help to bring in more of the love frequency. Please say this, 'I merge with all agreement to defend, avoid, separate from love as a protection. I merge with this decision wherever I made it, whenever I made it, so I would not kill and activate the dark shadows of my soul. I bless this decision. I call it into love. It was the best I could do.' Now breathe into the decision. It was the loving decision in the context of separation.

I repeat what Robin coaches me to say and breathe deeply. [In prior sessions, I had learned the power of releasing beliefs by owning why I created them and accepting them in my body. By merging with the belief and honoring how it served me, I then gain the power to transform it in my soul, personality, and imprint in my body.]

Robin: [Robin uses sound and clapping to move the energy in the space.] Are you ready to break that contract and experience whatever the consequences are?

Beth: Yes.

Robin: [Robin leads me through the declaration I must make to discreate the agreement.] Say, 'Through the power of love, I discreate all mechanisms, all devices, all decisions, all contracts to separate from love, to protect myself. I shatter this agreement in every dimension of my being.'

I repeat what Robin coaches me to say. [Sounds and clapping fill the space. My legs are vigorously kicking, and my arms are punching the space around me as I shatter the agreement, discharging energy out of my limbs.]

Robin: Now, everything you need to express can be loved, the darkest, the most poisonous, whatever you want to call it. All of the hatred, all of the programming to kill, all of it now can be revealed because love is holding a space for it. There is nothing that you expressed or can do that cannot be loved by God, that cannot be loved by us, and ultimately by yourself. Are you willing to call forth those aspects of the soul that did not believe they can be part of love?

Beth: I am.

Robin: What are you feeling in your body?

Beth: Just more sensation. The nausea has subsided.

Robin: So, there is an energetic switch that goes on when the love frequency comes into the body which is why you moved away from Daniel [a former boyfriend]. You probably avoided full bonding with your children, as well. So, understand, in the context of your experience, you have incredible love, that you could separate from the love, to protect and to allow the survival. At the highest level, there's immense love here; but the willingness to have it activate in the human body is what has been the separation. But now we can bring it straight in.

Beth: Yeah. [Tears begin to fill my eyes. My chest heaves up and down as I sob with compassion for the journey I have been on. My shoulders lower as I sink into the spaces inside of me that have been holding such pain.]

Robin: [Robin's hands are still on my body.] There you go. Just feel this acceptance that you have protected your children from your patterning, as best as you could. [Warm, soft tears run down my cheeks.] The love that it took to not activate fully with them and bond with them, so you would not hurt them physically… [was immense]. Forgive yourself now, right in this moment, for not bonding with them and activating the love frequency because there was a switch that went off in your being, as soon as you felt the love, the switch would go off, the impulse to kill would come out, and now that's where we need to go.

Beth: I remember Steven as a baby and that is when I think I found that switch. I recall physically making that decision not to throw him across the room (Chapter Seven). [I begin sobbing.] *Oh my god. It is miraculous that I overrode my programming. There was something good in me. I did not want to hurt my child.*

Robin: Go right into the grief, right into the body. And go right to that moment with your son. Go right into that moment where he is expressing emotion as a child. So, we merge now into that moment and feel that dark space. Your mind kicked in and stopped you from throwing the child. And go to the point before the mind kicked in. Go to the point of the emotions that were surfacing as he was screaming, and you were attempting to love him. [Robin uses specific sounds in her voice that have the purpose of breaking up and transmuting the controllers in spirit and the denial in my body.]

Beth: I remember being exhausted and having a terrible headache and going to sleep. Then when I woke up, the headache was gone.

Robin: And what are you feeling in your body, Sweetie?

Beth: I am just trying to breathe down into my belly.

[With the impulse to throw Steven across the room as a newborn infant, I had never forgotten what I had almost done to Steven. In this session, I was able to link the switch we had just identified to that memory. At the time of Steven's infancy, I had no clue as to what had happened; now I did. After all these years of healing work, I see that this was one of the conscious clues I unconsciously left for myself to help me discover the programming that was hidden from me. What we now understand about mind control programming is that through rituals they linked affection with violence. When I reached a certain love frequency through affection and bonding with family members, it was followed by torture. So subconsciously, I had a defense mechanism to stop the love frequency because immediately I anticipated torture and pain, and I was programmed to do violence to others, especially those I loved.]

[I needed to discreate the agreement to separate from love as a protection, so I could now safely allow love to be present to transmute the programming.]

DISCOVERING PROGRAMMING OF MY SPLIT PERSONALITY

The session continues.

Robin: I sense you are leaving your body [disassociating]. We are now in that moment of programming. It seems as if when the programming kicked in, you left your body and another aspect took over. We are right in the moment when you are trying to

99

leave the body. We need to reorganize this, so that you stay present. Say this, 'I call forth my presence throughout all memory. I am willing to stay and experience. I command through my will and the will of the One, full presence to integrate, remember, and observe and feel this other part of soul.'

I repeat what Robin coaches me to say.

Robin: [Robin continues to share her psychic perceptions.] So, what they did was a split personality with you so that you have absolutely no memory from one personality experience to the other. And you have not yet met this other part of your personality. It is also a soul part. It has come through in dreams, memories, impulses. So, what we are doing right now is we are integrating, we are making the unconscious, conscious. The shadow is rearing up right now, and it wants to take over, so I want you to look at me and we are going to create a boundary. Please tell it, 'I'm willing to allow you to speak through me but you can't take over. Because I've chosen to hold the Christ consciousness no matter what you are doing or what you are feeling.'

[Robin talks directly to this separated part in me.] 'I see you. I see you in Beth, and I know you think you are evil and more powerful than my love and more powerful than her love. But you do not frighten me, no matter what you think. You do not frighten me. My love is greater than your fear, and so is Beth's. You don't frighten me.' [Hearing Robin's words and fierceness, I am reassured that this separated force is not in control. I feel a willingness to let it speak through me.] You

100

have stayed separate from Beth, haven't you? Why did you do that? Why did you stay separate from her?

Beth: 'To stay hidden.' [I feel a frequency shift as the part answers.]

Robin: And where have you been living?

Beth: 'In the darkness.'

Robin: And you are here to talk now. What is different now?

Beth: 'The love is here. And I can't hurt anybody.'

Robin: And I will not let you hurt yourself. And we have Joseph here who understands the shadow and understands you. What were you taught to do?

Beth: 'To hurt, to cause as much pain as possible, to show the rage outwardly, to manifest it, to make it a physical reality.'

Robin: You are doing great, Beth. [Then Robin addresses the part that thinks it is Satan.] Do you have a name? What did they call you when you were in the middle [center] of the violence?

Beth: Lucifer.

Robin: Lucifer, Child of Lucifer, Angel of Lucifer? Can you feel that? Satan? Lucifer? Right now, you are talking to me. Are you also feeling your anger or are you able to just watch it right now?

Beth: [I answer for this part.] 'I can just watch it.' [Joseph is coughing heavily.]

Robin: Do you understand that you have been manipulated? Did you know that? Lucifer part, do you know that you are just part of the manipulation?

Beth: 'I don't think [I knew that]. I think I thought I had my own… it was just me so I could stay in shame.'

Joseph: I am picking up on a lot of the terror and threats to kill you that are in your field. I think we need a soul retrieval here.

[I began to understand how completely manipulated and split I was, having had no inkling of what had been perpetrated upon me until these sessions. As I was getting validation through my physical sensations that there was physical torture, the amount of terror and depression I had always had along with my robotic existence started making complete sense. I was welling up with self-compassion as Robin and Joseph witnessed the truth of my life.]

DECONSTRUCTING THE PROGRAMMING AND SOUL RETRIEVAL

The session continues.

Robin: We need to unwind [help make conscious] what the threat was if she remembered and told the story. 'What did they tell you would happen if you told the truth?'

Beth: 'They would chop me in little pieces and other people that I loved. And I personally would be responsible for a massacre.'

Robin: They felt that they could control this part to come out whenever they wanted it to, because, were you signaled by sound or numbers or how would they signal you?

Beth: I guess sound. They told me they would make me come out and kill my family, and it would be at a time like the daytime, a place not in the darkness.

Robin: And they had a way of mind controlling you, they had captured your will. Is your will evil if somebody else had captured it?

Beth: No. [I begin to cry.] I did not want to do it. It is so unfair. Unfair is not even the word. [Robin claps loudly into the space.]

Robin: [To Joseph] Can you hold presence above her body and lower down her soul part? I feel this part of the soul is trying to come in.

Robin: [To Beth] The spiritual field and matrix grids Joseph is creating are of health and truth, making it possible and safe for this part to show up. The space cannot be controlled by fear, but fear is welcome to move here with love [in your body].

Beth: I was always scared, wondering what it [my unconscious part] had done that I did not know about even as an adult.

Robin: And now you are going to know. You will not be split anymore, Sweetheart. So, tell this part, 'you won't be split anymore. I have enough love and support to integrate. I have enough strength to integrate.'

I repeat what Robin coaches me to say.

Robin: I psychically hear its voice, and it is saying, 'who would want to integrate me?' Now Beth, look in my eyes. Okay, now you are starting to go out of your body, and I hear, 'I want to die'. Can you feel that?

Beth: Yeah. I feel I want to leave.

Robin: Okay. Beth, I want you to say to this part, 'I can love you in the horror. I am not going to cast you out no matter what you have to tell me, because you are part of me, and I'm here to heal violence in my soul and on this planet. There is a deeper purpose here, and the judgment of you has kept us separate.'

I repeat what Robin coaches me to say. Energy is moving through my body. I feel apathy in my heart and limbs.

Robin: Okay. There you go. We are going to release the judgment because this soul part cannot integrate until we release the judgment. Please repeat with me, 'From the power of God that I am and the Oneness of all time, space, and dimension, I merge with the separation, the violence, where we have judged violence, judged killing as separate from God, I merge with this judgment.' [Deep guttural noises come forth from Robin and me. Robin expresses her sound healing.] 'All identification that violence is evil, we merge into this matrix now.' You have enough love, Beth, to come through this. 'All identification that violence is evil and separate from God, I merge into this matrix where humanity has not been able to heal violence because it has not brought it home into love and forgiveness.'

I repeat what Robin coaches me to say. Robin continues to use her sound healing to bring forth the love frequency into the violence. I am making guttural noises.

Robin: Okay, we are ready now to dissolve the judgment. Joseph, please join with us. 'I discreate all judgment, all separation, that violence is not God, that violence cannot be loved by God, that violence is Satan. I discreate these judgments, these condemnations, this identification.' Breathe. Breathe. Breathe. 'And we call forth the power of God to integrate, to embrace violence in the circle of love, for compassion.'

I repeat what Robin coaches me to say.

[In order to heal a fractured part, it has to come fully back into the body. That is the purpose of soul retrieval, but I could not allow it to take me over. So, we had to create a non-judgmental, loving space within me that would accept with compassion what the programmed part had done, before we could bring the part in. During that process, I learn about their threats to trigger me into violence if I tell what was happening. Robin reminds me that they had captured my will and I had had no choice, affirming that I need to have compassion for myself. **The acknowledgement that violence and killing are actually part of God is the key to removing the separation.** Being separated from this part keeps me from healing it. When I call on God's love for those parts, then I can heal.]

THE LOST CHILD

The session continues.

Robin: Breathing in. That is it, Beth. Now look at that soul part. How old is it when it began to believe it was separate from God?

Beth: Three or four.

Robin: Say, 'hello, you've been talking through me. Thank you. I am ready to let you express now. What makes you believe you are unlovable?'

I repeat what Robin coaches me to say.

Beth: 'I kill. I torture. I hurt.'

Robin: And they told you [that] you were evil because of this?

Beth: 'Uh huh. They loved it. They said that is what love was. That's what they celebrated.'

Robin: Did they love it or were they addicted to it?

Beth: [My adult self is now responding.] They were addicted to it.

Robin: So, we are really talking to your soul here, Beth, not the child, and that is okay. Did they tell you that you loved it too?

Beth: Yeah.

Robin: Were you really good at it? Were you a good little girl and did whatever they said?

Beth: Yes.

Robin: And they celebrated you for that, didn't they? Keep breathing that in. Did you get a sense of power from that, being worshipped?

Beth: [Responding from my little girl self.] Yeah.

Robin: You enjoyed that, didn't you? Did you miss out on receiving love in other ways? It made you hungry for attention, didn't it? So, can you see, Beth, how the little child was made so vulnerable because it couldn't bond through true love with the mother and the father, it was vulnerable to being swept up into the adoration of the group? [I felt impulses in my arms and solar plexus moving outward as Robin spoke to me. My head felt a tingly heat as I realized that part of me had liked being celebrated this way.] So, look on the child and say, 'Your needs were not getting met, so you looked anywhere for energy.

106

Energy, love, and attention were all the same to you, even negative energy was better than nothing.'

I repeat what Robin coaches me to say.

Robin: And breathing down into the body. Are you willing to see now how they programmed you to hurt, what they had to do in your body, and start to move that pain out?

Beth: Yes.

Robin: Say, 'I call back the part of my child that holds the pain in her body, that holds the memory of the pain and the actions to create pain. I call you back. I call you forth. I call you home.' [This is called conscious soul retrieval.]

I repeat what Robin coaches me to say.

[As I speak to the little child, my adult self realizes how extremely devoid of recognition, attention and love I was during childhood. I can see why I would have welcomed attention of any sort. A deep wave of sadness and compassion washes over me.]

INTEGRATION INTO THE HEART SANCTUARY

The session continues.

Robin: Now see the house [in your inner sanctuary] with the [inner] mother and tell this little girl she is going to be able to be healed in this new house. [In an earlier session, I had created an inner sanctuary with a home in my heart.] Tell her, as she comes into your body, 'We are going to get a new home so that your body can heal. You are not going to go through torture again, but it's time to feel it and show me what happened.'

I repeat what Robin coaches me to say.

Robin: Say, 'I merge with my three-year old. Come home. Come home. You are not evil. I discreate all judgment of you as evil. You are part of God, [that is] lost.' [Sound healing] That is it and breathing right down here. [Robin's hand is on my belly.] So, you were triggered into violence when you started loving, so we need to unweave that. Joseph, what are you observing here? It feels like there is an etheric code or something. Is this the actual switch that turns on when the love frequency is activated in the body? Are you seeing the mechanism? Are you being veiled, Joseph?

Joseph: The field is so thick and heavy. It is just like mud. It comes and it goes.

Robin: And what are you feeling, Beth, in your body now?

Beth: I can feel my bladder.

I take a bathroom break and am thinking about how my survival is miraculous. I am amazed that I have not "gone crazy" and ended up in a mental institution.

Beth: [Returning] I guess some people go crazy from all of this.

Robin: Yes, people do. And you were not willing to activate your memories until you had the right support. We [meaning Robin, Joseph, and I] have committed to hold love and unity for both shadow and light. And that is how wise your soul is in relationship to your purpose, because you did not come in here to go crazy. You came in here to serve the healing.

[One of the most powerful tools I learned in my sessions was my power to create loving spaces in my heart to meet the needs of my retrieved inner children.]

I lie down so we can continue our work, and I go into the breath.

DISCOVERING MECHANISMS THAT TRIGGERED PROGRAMMING TO KILL

The session continues.

Robin: We are going to go right to that mechanism, that device, wherever it is. [Robin goes into prayer.] Great Spirit, we ask now to be shown these devices in the etheric and in the body and these implants that were placed in this field, so whenever the love frequency and the bonding in the emotional body began to happen, the switch would go off to kill, to harm, to maim, and we ask now through the power of the love and the light to expand the consciousness into all realms so that we can see and feel where this is living in Beth. Beth, say, 'I merge with this mechanism, this implant, whatever it may be within myself, in any part of my soul, if I love I'll kill, if I love I'll kill, if I love I'll kill [Robin uses sound healing]. I'm a good girl if I kill, I'm a good girl if I kill, if I love I kill.'

I repeat what Robin coaches me to say.

[I keep repeating the phrase, and I move into a frenzied high pitch voice with energy surging through my body. My arms are flailing in the air, rage pouring forth with these words. I am stabbing invisible beings, releasing the coupling that love means killing. Robin and Joseph are transmuting these energies through sound healing and energy work.]

Robin: Say, 'I dissolve all devices programmed into my being, into my etheric, emotional body, if I love I will kill. I discreate this now. I shatter this device now. I call on Spirit now. We transmute, we transmute, we transmute this illusion and linkup.' It is right down there in the bladder. And [you can express] whatever emotional energy, whatever words that want to come out. Joseph's going to put his hands right here and he is going to push, he is going to really go in there [with energy, where the device is].

[With my permission, Joseph places his hands over my bladder and starts sending energy into my bladder.]

Robin: Great Spirit, we ask now, purify, purify, purify, purify all mechanisms, all devices in the organs, in the bladder, in the bone, in the blood [sound healing]. Look at the baby body and how they started programming her with a probe up the baby vagina. Can you see that? Just try to sink in and call her forth. Tell her, 'You were programmed to do these things, you were forced. They tricked you. You are not evil. Show me now how they did it. Let me feel so my body can get free.'

I repeat what Robin coaches me to say.

110

[I learned that mechanisms could be placed in my energy field in my etheric body to control me. This was new information at that time. I have come to understand how much we humans are influenced by energies and forces outside of our awareness. This lack of awareness is what kept me split and was my strategy of survival.]

[Joseph connects to my soul vibration by using his hands and he guides this soul part physically from four feet above my body into my body. Once the child is brought into my body, I have access to my rage. I feel this energy and my body starts to discharge as my limbs flail about. We work with dissolving the mechanism which is in my bladder. As we dismantle the mechanism, I continue to discharge rage. Joseph puts healing energy into my bladder and so do I. At this point, I realized that so much of me was residing outside of my body and that it was possible to bring these parts back in through soul retrieval.]

The session continues.

Robin: Try to breathe into Joseph's hand and as deeply into the bladder as you can. That is it. So, I am seeing in the four-year old, whenever you would start doing something loving, they would give you a shock, a pain. They did this conditioning. What did they give you when you were actually able to hurt an animal or hurt a child? What did they do for you? Drugs?

Beth: Cookies. The chocolate chip cookies.

Robin: Okay. Breathe into that. Tell her, 'You got rewarded with sugar and pleasure when you hurt others. And what happened when you were loving?'

I repeat what Robin coaches me to say.

Beth: [Speaking for the child] 'I got hurt. They stuck that thing inside me.' [I feel a huge wave of rage welling up, and my arms flail about; I want to destroy anyone who comes near me.]

Robin: Are you seeing that Joseph?

Joseph: I am feeling it. I am feeling the violation.

Robin: We are going to go back and as Joseph moves the energy out of the little girl, I want you to see the four-year old and say, 'I'm from the future, and we are going to take this probe out and we are going to get you away from this. You were taught that to kill is pleasure, to feel good in killing, and you were taught that to love is painful.'

I repeat what Robin coaches me to say.

[The deconditioning process of the child comes when we understand with love in our hearts how this confusion was created through a reward/punishment or pleasure/pain cycle. My child was fractured in many parts. Some parts stayed in my own physical body in my bladder and vagina. Other parts were stuck in an etheric dimension, often astral, which then requires a conscious intention to retrieve that part of me and join it with other parts of the same age of that traumatized child.]

BRINGING THE FRACTURED CHILD INTO PRESENT TIME

Robin: So, we are going to discreate these matrices, these consciousness patterns, and then we are going to rescue her out of there. Actually, I think we need to get her out of there first, then we will discreate.

So, see where she is and see what they are doing now with that probe. [At this point, we are actually learning how to move through time to retrieve the child out of the past physical/emotional place where her consciousness is stuck. This is called soul retrieval. Joseph is explaining to me that he is opening up energy portals so I can access my own child's consciousness.]

Now, from the future, Beth, you are going to go to her from the future and say, 'I'm here. I'm taking her now.' [A sense of relief is calming me. The feeling of wanting to kill is subsiding.]

I repeat what Robin coaches me to say.

[I feel my little girl is in a separate time and separate space from my physical body. I start to feel a vibrational connection to my little girl when Robin coaches me to pick her up.]

Robin: Pick her up. Pick her up. That is it. Now run away. Run, run, run, run, run. Jump through the time/light portal to present time. That is it and go down the path and say now, 'I call forth my guides to help me heal my child. Mother Mary, Yeshua, all the beings of love and healing, Metatron, Kyron, all the beings to heal my electromagnetic field in my emotional body, in my physical body.'

[Robin continues to guide me. With my eyes closed, I feel my child vibrating into my body more.]

Robin: Now open into a safe environment. Open into this beautiful golden light. Take this child, this four-year old. There she is. Now this is the part that is done the killing. Let her express whatever she wants now that you are holding her, now that she is safe. Breathe into her. What does she want to tell you? Adult self, when those are the only choices a child has, to be tortured or to have sugar and pleasure, what is the child going to choose?

Beth: Sugar and pleasure.

Robin: To survive, because that is the natural instinct, isn't it?

Beth: [I feel a dull throbbing pain in my vagina spreading out in a spider pattern. My adult self is shocked to know how they treated my little girl. I need verification.] They tortured her until she would agree to kill?

Uncoupling Conditioning that Linked Sugar Pleasure with the Action of Killing

Robin: Yes. Feel that now. Feel that, Beth. Now let the little girl go into your arms. That is it. She is not evil, Beth. She was tortured into it. Say, 'I discreate all perception that if I kill, that I'll get pleasure. I discreate this conditioning. I shatter this now out of the little girl. I no longer allow this association, this linkup that killing equals pleasure, fulfillment, and reward. I dissolve this conditioning now.'

I repeat what Robin coaches me to say. [I feel courage in my belly. I have a firm, strong resolve to unlink the conditioning. I feel my will and determination, my strength coming back in.]

Robin: Say, 'You don't have to kill to get pleasure. Keep telling her. You do not have to kill to get attention, to get praise, to get love. That is not how we do it now. And you were not a bad girl. You were doing the only thing that you could do to survive.' [My breath deepens with the realization of how I was manipulated and that I am not essentially evil.]

I repeat what Robin coaches me to say.

Robin: Do you have regret that you chose to survive? Can you feel how confused she is about choosing to live? So, she has hated the fact that she chose to survive. Can you feel that confusion? Tell her, 'You have enough love to survive through all this. Thank you for surviving.'

I repeat what Robin coaches me to say. [I can feel a breath of awe descend through my body as I realize that I have survived this torture.]

Robin: Feel your heart now and just hug that four-year old. [Robin hands me a pillow to hug.] Hug her so tight and say, 'Thank you for surviving. That was a great choice. Without you surviving, I could not fulfill our purpose. You are so strong. You are so beautiful.'

[I continue to comfort my four-year old, bathing her in my compassion. She is naked, alone, and cold, so I provide clothing and warmth to her in my inner sanctuary. I tell her, "I love you no matter what you had to do. You did it to survive. I forgive you. Thank you for surviving." I assure her that she is not evil. We continue energy work to heal her bladder and dissolve the killing impulses. I acknowledge in the present moment that if I had not survived, I could not have awakened and healed these ritual abuse patterns in my family line.]

115

DISCUSSION

This session exposed the satanic energies that were in my energy field and revealed how they were programmed to operate through me. This understanding of how my system had been hijacked laid the foundation for my commitment to go from unconscious memories to conscious awareness, so that my love became the healing agent. Love with Source, my soul, myself, became the healing agent. After the parts came into my system, they could be deprogrammed; you cannot deprogram something that is not first integrated. Integration did not mean that fragments would stay in my system programmed to kill. I had to make the commitment to integrate these energies and repair and transform them. Robin and Joseph were often in a prayerful, healing state while working with me, receiving this information for the first time. They were learning along with me.

The Intensive was the perfect container to express everything that had been locked down inside of me: to draw, to move, to dance, to scream, to cry, to feel. It helped me understand more fully the denial of how much trauma my body had gone through. The denial began to peel away as I expressed and sounded. Without my soul on board wanting to get the learning and to take responsibility for helping my body heal, I probably would have gone mentally ill. I began to experience how the love frequency was the answer to healing everything, no matter how vile.

When we worked together in the weeks before the Intensive, I had uncovered my three-year old's memories of being consistently raped by my father in our home. I had retrieved this part of me that was disassociated, and it was through the integration that I had full body memory. I remembered that my sister Dawn, at an earlier point in time, had also revealed that she was raped by my father. I began to defrost the numb, invisible child who felt like she was dead and in a coffin.

Subsequent sessions during the Intensive revealed how satanic programming was implemented, and I began to access my rage and understand that my rage is a natural human reaction to torture. I felt my compassion come forward for myself as I realized I had survived horrific torture, and the "choices" I had been given were not choices at all. During one session, Robin had handed me a baby doll and asked me to show her what had happened. I began beating and poking the doll. My arms punched and pounded. Deep groaning, growling, menacing noises filled the space, and the desire to attack was coursing through my veins. Soon the head of the baby doll flew across the room as my rage was unleashed. I was re-enacting the rage and hatred that my perpetrators had created by electroshocking my vagina; they placed a knife into my hand guiding me to discharge my rage by killing an innocent animal. I could finally access my rage in a safe, contained environment and allow it to heal through my own compassionate heart.

By repeating so much of the dialog with my voice, I got to feel where these beliefs were living in my body. If, at any time, my body had not felt validated, I would have discontinued the sessions. But over time, each session brought me more awareness, memories, connection, grounding, emotional truth, and presence. I was able to feel more love and that felt good. I wanted to continue.

When I later shared my processes with Dawn, she also validated how the programming lived in her body through her aches and pains. We ultimately realized that once we embraced the sensations, they would move through our bodies gracefully, and we would come out of suffering. Dawn and I committed to doing part of our session work together which validated the experiences of our lives.

FOUNDATIONAL SPIRITUAL PRINCIPLES FOR HEALING

This Intensive laid a foundation for the principles that continue to guide my healing in the present. Some of those principles are stated below.

- I am a sovereign being with the power of love to create and discreate through my consciousness in my body and soul.

- By claiming personal responsibility for my life through my soul and personality, I enroll and attract tremendous love and support from spirit, my environment, community, and healers.

- Satanic energies are parts of the Oneness that have forgotten they belong to love. They have chosen to experience power and control instead of oneness. Love can embrace satanic energies which dismantles their power to dominate.

- Through the frequency of love and connection to my soul power, I am able to discreate any contracts, beliefs, and agreements I have made that no longer serve me. I have parts of my soul that hold love and parts that do not. I was programmed to reject the parts of my soul that held love.

- Many parts of my soul hold the desire for love and repair; I must consciously allow those parts into my human body.

- Programming can be dismantled with love over time, making a personal commitment to stay with one process, building a trusting rapport with the same facilitators and spiritual allies in a safe and loving environment.

- You cannot heal what you are not willing to feel.

- Deprogramming involves understanding that I create beliefs based on past experiences, so by merging with that choice (belief) with love and compassion, I then have the power to discreate the belief.

- I cannot transform anything I judge. Transformation of those beliefs must happen in my body tissue by merging with the moment they were formed. Then I have the power to discreate them from my emotional, physical, and spiritual planes.

- Judgment and denial are strategies of the satanic and separation forces on this earth. Blame, punishment, and arrogant righteousness disempower the love field. As I come out of denial and judgment of myself, my soul parts can come back into my body.

- In order to heal, a paradox needs to be embraced. I have to love (accept) my soul's choice to go through this learning, because if I judge myself or my experience, I will shut down the healing process. My soul has to love its choice to bring the traumatic experiences to itself through my current life circumstances and go through this learning for its evolutionary healing.

- I am not just healing myself and this life. This process includes all lifetimes of my soul, whether I was playing the role of victim, victimizer, or rescuer.

- My soul's timing was very specific, so that my memories would not come forth until I had a unity field and community support in which to embrace my trauma in safety and deprogram my psyche.

- In the healing journey, when we come out of denial, we often feel worse before we feel better.

- Once the dark emotional states are embraced, they have a cycle of completion through the tissue, that increases my capacity to feel love, joy, gratitude, and pleasure in my body.

Neither Robin, Joseph, nor I knew what my life would be like after the Intensive. Beforehand, I wondered if we could "get it all" and do away with the darkness in one fell swoop. Now, I just smile at that statement. How naïve I was. Slowly, I realized that there was no quick fix and that my healing journey had only begun. Robin and Joseph, also, report that they did not know, at that time, the extent of the work that we would do together or the time period that it would require.

Currently I can look back at the Intensive in 2003 and see it laid the foundation of my ability to trust the spiritual healing process. It established a resource within me that I had not found until I worked with Robin and Joseph at that time. I created a touchstone within myself of the essential quality of my healing journey.

Immediately after the Intensive, the effects were more subtle than I had hoped. In the early stages I would compartmentalize my sessions as separate from everyday life, and I would question whether anything was different in my life. But then a wave of good feelings would wash over me, and I would know that a new, pleasurable imprint had indeed taken root in my psyche and body. During the Intensive, I felt loved and cared for, like a kindergartener in a safe home. The imprint of feeling loved and cared for had been initiated when Robin was able to vibrate love when I was in trauma; she modeled that love so I could see how to give love to my inner children. The sandwich that she made me for lunch was so wonderful because I was open to receiving love after my wounded child had been brought back into my heart. Those good feelings were now part of me and were supporting a sense of well-being. My fragmented three/four-year old was integrating and receiving love in my heart, and the unconscious threat that any bonding and love would lead to trauma was being unwound and dismantled. I looked forward to seeing how I would relate to my family members. I was hoping for more expressed love in my life.

It took time for my healing experiences to integrate into new attitudes and behaviors in my life. During the Intensive, I had cracked open a foundational level of buried emotions and sensations that needed to be loved. *I hate myself. I hate my life.* Waves of emotion were now coming forth in place of the numbness which was my old and familiar state of being. A couple of days later, unexpectedly, feelings of emotional well-being would follow. *I feel deeply peaceful. Where did this come from?* If I gave into blame, then feelings of being trapped and powerless would take over and hook me back into being controlled by the satanic forces. *I feel bad but I will soon be completely healed.* But as time passed and I continued to feel more and more layers, I learned about my personal healing cycle.

"Dawn, I can't believe that I can feel such intense emotional pain and then feel real love and joy. Today, I actually felt like talking with some of the women in my exercise class." Then a few weeks later, depression would slip in. *Oh yeah, Robin says that depression is me suppressing my feelings. What do I need to feel now? I will call Robin and Joseph for a session.*

LIVING THE HEALING PATH

As I look back, integrating transformation that occurs during a session into a daily practice of more self-love is a great challenge. The Intensive has opened the doorway for the healing to happen. I have assignments to complete and they require commitment and discipline. I am supposed to listen to the recorded sessions. *Good lord. That is going to take forever… well, several days for sure.* As I take the time to listen, I feel more compassion for my little self that experienced the trauma. I need to be reminded of the new reality that I am creating as I dissolve the old beliefs, such as *I am not worthy.* One week after the sessions end, I am feeling sad and alone. I close my eyes and notice the thoughts in my head. *I do not know if my life will ever get better. I feel too sad to be around people.* I realize that these are the thoughts and feelings of my inner child, and I need to ask her what she needs. (We call this dialoging.) She tells me that she just wants to be with me and have a nice, warm bath. I can see her in my heart now, and I whisper to her. *Come be with me. You are not alone.* I draw a bath and enjoy the warm water with her. I am continuing to bond with her and keep her soul vibration with me. When we come out of the bath, we cuddle together under the soft covers of my bed. In a little while, I prepare her favorite meal, a grilled cheese sandwich. I feel her appreciation and acceptance of me as her new mother.

One of my assignments at the conclusion of my first Intensive is to practice energy work. I bring in from the higher dimensions ("up above") an energy of golden light into my body and send it down through my feet into Mother Earth; then I open to receive a silver energy from the Earth and join these energies in my body, creating a beautiful flow of golden and silver energies. I can feel the energy of light, life and love healing my body. My body is aware of the violation that I have uncovered. I feel an achy pain in my anus. I breathe into my pain and send a focused sound into it. It works. After a few minutes, the pain subsides.

I have days where I just want to be rocked. Some of the needs of my inner child can be met by imagining creating what she is asking for in my heart sanctuary. I invite the spiritual power of Mother God to soothe and rock my child as much as my little one needs and wants. My body relaxes as I absorb this comfort.

One of my favorite parts of integrating is receiving pleasurable touch without harm. I schedule a massage and enjoy the imprint that I am lovable. As I am lying there on the massage table and telling the therapist what I need, I notice that my voice is a pitch that is higher than usual. *My little girl has a voice!*

CHAPTER THIRTEEN

Learning to Love My Needs

I am anxious to share what I have experienced with Dawn. I invite her over. "I want to tell you about my Intensive. I uncovered memories about the torture and how I was trained to kill. My rage was so intense, and I felt so incredibly helpless."

"I know, Beth. What we have gone through is shocking. Most of the time I can't stand to think about it."

"I was so enraged that as I was acting out a memory, the baby doll's head came off and flew across the room. I do not know how we survived. It's a miracle."

"Our nightlife was absolutely terrifying."

"You know, Dawn, I finally have begun to really understand why it is so hard for me to take risks and try new things. Life has always felt precarious to me. For most of my life, I did not even understand it was my job to take care of my own needs. I did not really know what needs were, that I had them, and that I was supposed to take care of myself that way. I did not know that that was possible until Robin taught me how to comfort my traumatized inner children. It is challenging to figure out what I need day in and day out. How do you figure out what you need, Dawn?"

"Well, sometimes I just act 'as if' I know, imitating what I have seen others do," she replies. "I don't always know how I feel or what fun is."

"I still struggle to make sense of my feelings, too. Sometimes I wish I had someone to take care of me all the time. Now I have to be my own mother."

Dawn's face is etched with sadness. It is hard to face the facts of our lives, and when we do, we can only stand to feel the grief in small doses. However, I also can feel her relief in knowing that I am now fully embracing what she has been trying to share with me for years. I am finally validating Dawn. I look at her. My heart smiles. We are becoming allies.

"Even though I have to work hard to know what my needs are, Dawn, I am willing to be vulnerable and figure things out, one step at a time. I do know that I like to dance. I want to focus on that."

"Why don't you come with me this Wednesday?" Dawn has been part of a dance community for over a decade. "That's one way I have found to connect with people, and I have become part of that group by consistently showing up."

"Okay," I say. "If I know you are going, that will help me get myself out the door." I feel excited with the possibility of enjoying myself.

We enter the dimly lit establishment and make our way over to the tables where the dancers gather. I look to see who I know. *A few of the guys that I have danced with before are here.* I notice a playfulness emerging in me wanting to interact with other people.

Ron approaches me with a smile. He extends his hand, and his head leans toward the dance floor, an invitation to join him. I smile and nod; soon we are scooting around the floor doing the two-step. *I am actually a fairly good dancer.* I hear myself ask myself why I am so hesitant. And then I acknowledge my trauma. *Oh yeah, I am terrified of connection.*

Dawn and I continue our conversation the next day. "Sometimes I actually feel like I hate my needs," I say. "They seem like a big bother. Guess what I discovered the other day? I closed my eyes and asked the child in me why I hated needing anything. This is what my five-year old revealed to me."

I am outside, and it is very dark. I do not know where I am, and my head feels funny. I have been in the cold for what seems like forever. I am alone. I am hungry. I gotta pee. My legs are wobbly as I try to stay upright. A pseudo-friendly, deep voice from an unidentified male is telling me that I have a chance to show them how special I am. "We just want you to show us who you really are," the voice says. Every time I start to fall, I am prodded by a sharp poke in my back.

"Stand up and stay awake," I say to my exhausted, foggy self. I look down and see my filthy arms.

Light shines brightly into my eyes, blinding me, and I hear, "Are you ready? Are you ready to show us who you really are?"

I nod as dizziness envelops my head. My body shivers. Warm pee trickles down my leg creating a small puddle at my feet. My knees buckle, and I fall to the ground. "You stupid, stinking girl. Maybe we are wrong about you. Maybe you are not as smart as we thought. Go back and think about who you really are. If you are lucky, you can have another chance to prove yourself later." Someone drags me away from the spotlight.

I am small. I have no voice. There is only more punishment if I cry out. I am being deprived of all my physical needs. I am terrified. There is no one to call to for help. I feel hopeless.

The cycles of deprivation continue in this training. Finally, a masked figure walks me out again to the center of the circle. I feel an electric shock go through my body, radiating out from the center of my back, behind my heart. Blinding rage fills my brain, and I am no longer weak. Someone puts a knife in my hand, providing an outlet for my blinding rage. As this energy pulses through my body, I begin to thrust the knife, stabbing what is before me. I hear animals squealing, and it all becomes a cacophony of sound, rage, and liquid. My rage releases and I am spent.

"Good," a voice says calmly. "Now we see who you are. You are Satan's child. We know that we can count on you to show us who you really are." I am rewarded with warmth and chocolate chip cookies and rest and comfort and praise for my killing. I hated my needs. Having needs meant being manipulated and controlled. My strategy was to have no needs so I could have a small illusion of power in this circumstance.

There is a heavy space between us as I finish sharing my memory. Dawn's righteous anger speaks. "How could we possibly know anything about meeting needs when we lived in survival mode? We had to numb ourselves. This is how people get programmed to do inhuman acts because they are robotic, unfeeling and without needs. It has been impossible to admit basic needs, even between us. They just didn't exist for us."

We are more a team now. I feel some of my hurt and resistance dropping as we hug each other for a very long time. The wall I had resurrected to never trust my sister is crumbling.

"Dawn, do you think we can actually become human now?"

Dawn looks at me as the possibilities for our lives become promising. "I won't have to just copy everyone around me," she says. "I now can discover what I want."

A sense of excitement about living a fulfilling life is bubbling up inside of me. "What do you think of inviting some women for a processing group with Robin? I ask. "I'd like to host it in my home."

"Well, it's the best work on the planet if you really want to heal your stuff," Dawn declares. "I have some women in mind to invite."

Soon I am enjoying the group of women that we have gathered together. "Do you notice how powerful it is to work in a group? We seem to be able to move a lot of energy when there is a unified field created by several women. I always look forward to group night. If I am depressed, I know I can address my issues there and get results." I had quit taking antidepressants now that I had more access to my suppressed emotions.

Some of this group wanted to create fun and adventure. "Who wants to go to Arkansas to dig for crystals?" one woman asked. Many of us were lovers of crystals and their capacity to support healing.

"I don't know about digging for crystals. That sounds like a lot of hard work. But I would love to go to the gem shows," I responded.

A two-car caravan headed for Arkansas. Gems and minerals were on display for wholesale prices. A powerful piece of quartz crystal was calling to me from the table. I headed over and picked it up. "Ouch." My pointer finger was bleeding. I heard an inner voice say, *Initiation. Oh, I am entering a new phase in my life with crystals and their capacity to support my healing.*

"Hey Dawn. Look what I found. It is a smoky quartz. I can feel it is my power crystal." As we stopped at other places along the way, other beauties spoke to me, and I brought many of them home.

Dawn and I kept looking for things to do together. "Have you tried essential oils? A friend of mine is doing a class this Saturday." Dawn was hoping I would go with her.

I do love essential oils. Yes, let's do it."

We are sitting at a table deeply smelling essential oils. The teacher tells us about the wonderful properties of each oil. Lemon. Orange. Lavender. Thyme. *I feel high when I breathe in these oils.* We focus on the oil, Ylang Ylang. We are told, "This sweet-scented oil can produce euphoria and, therefore, could enhance a loving relationship." I look at Dawn. We both smile. *I will have to buy some of that one, for sure.* A burst of joy bubbles up from my solar plexus. *I am so glad we are here together.* Now our love was rebuilding in a way that it never could before.

"Beth, I know I've hurt you. I have had mental and emotional flashbacks of that. I've felt so guilty and ashamed; I haven't wanted to be close to you." Dawn's confession reaches deep into my heart. Later we would retrieve memories that explained why we had never been close before, discovering that we had been intentionally trained to hurt one another. How amazing it is that we are both now willing to find our way out of the hatred together and not blame one another for what happened.

CHAPTER FOURTEEN

I Want Wholeness but I Have Been Programmed

It is 2007, and I can actually notice growth in me. I am starting to acknowledge my needs and get them met consistently for the first time in my life. I realize that my soul's evolution involves learning how to repair as much as I can inside of me with my inner children, which leads me to wanting to work with parents and children in the world. So, I learn compassionate communication skills and end up teaching them at a class in a church. I want to be part of healing families, anywhere I can. I continue to explore different forms of dance and movement, dismantling the rigidity in my muscles; and art is a place where I can let out my unconscious feelings and learn more about myself. My healing journey now is creating more aliveness, desires, and joys, experiences of taking risks, and finding out how healthy my creative energies are. Through different activities I am learning how to socialize and have new friends and some of them are men. The purpose of my life now is about becoming whole! I choose to move closer to my healing community.

In my new environment, I begin to ponder who I would be in an intimate relationship now that I have been doing healing work for more than four years. *I wonder if I could have a healthy relationship with a man. Who would want to be with me after I tell him that I was brought up in a satanic cult where I was tortured, violated sexually and fragmented? I would love to do sexual healing with a partner, but who the hell would be willing? Maybe someone on their own healing path. Perhaps I could have a conscious loving relationship where, if I were triggered from touch, I could breathe through it and not have my numbness ruin the relationship. Is that even possible for me?*

I am starting to notice that I am being drawn romantically to certain men. And although Don is my friend, I also find him attractive. He has a handsome face with Greek features framed by silvery gray hair. He loves to talk and sees himself as an expert. He even wants to start a match-making business. I have a crush on him. He asks to meet with me to discuss helping him write a book. Because of our friendship and the mutual healers that we both associate with, he already knows about my traumatic experiences.

I decide to take a big risk of self-disclosure. I say, "How would you feel about working with someone who has a crush on you?"

Don changes the subject. As we near the end of our meeting, he suggests, "Let's get some dinner sometime." *I wonder what 'get dinner' means. Is he asking me out?*

A few days later, we are sitting across from one another in a restaurant. I can feel my insecurity about anyone ever wanting to be with me. As I listen to Don, he says, "I think total honesty in sharing feelings is very important in a relationship." He asks me many questions requiring me to share how I feel and identify what my needs are.

I am flooded with numbness. I feel the pressure of him wanting a specific answer. *What if I do not tell him what he wants to hear? Will he reject me? I actually do not know how I feel. Yikes.*

"This is too much for me, Don. I just don't have answers for all these questions." I have only recently been learning about conscious relationships. We abandon the discussion, and after dinner go for a walk. *I do not think this is going to turn into anything.*

The next morning, he calls. "It was pure magic last night." I am in shock with his assessment. *What is he talking about? I guess he liked the part where we cuddled in his car after the walk. I was ready to let it go but he seems interested.*

This small bit of attention from Don is like a drug in my system. I begin spending more and more time at his house. We enjoy kissing and making out. I feel wanted. I start to think that maybe he will be the one that can help me heal sexually. Even though I had that thought, I did not know how to ask for his presence in helping me heal, allowing me to feel my body in a new way during sexual experiences. Before I knew it, we were having sex. It was as if we slid down a hormonal slope before I realized that I had not even *chosen* to have sex with him. One part of me was already having sex with him while another part of me was totally unsure about the relationship. But there I was, in a rhythm and pattern of saying *yes* because it was the only way I knew how to connect with a man.

Not long after we connect, Don announces, "I have to go to the UK on business for several weeks. Would you be willing to housesit and take care of my dog?"

"Sure, no problem." I move in to housesit, and when he returns, I stay.

For the first couple months after his return, we spend most mornings in bed, sharing visions of the future and having sex. He starts seeing me in his future, and I start to feel joy that someone is choosing me. I have never been happier. I feel aroused and open to sexual exploration every morning. My veins are pulsating with something that makes me feel euphoric. Sex with each other is like a drug that fascinates both of us. We cannot get enough. One time, as we gaze in each other's eyes, I see Don shiver. "What's up?" I ask.

"I guess I am a little bit scared of you. I'm not sure exactly what it is, but I sense something powerful," he replies. I notice my thoughts. *Good. I want sexual power over Don.* I question whether my sexual attraction to Don is from my heart.

And then one morning Don pulls away and does not want to touch me. He asks me, "What are you feeling?"

I start to feel anxiety moving up my body. I do not know what I am feeling. Our pattern of making love in the morning has been broken. Feelings are emerging. I instantly think to myself that something is wrong with me because he does not want to have sex with me.

This is the first big rupture in our drug-induced bliss. We seek Robin and Joseph's help, and I learn that my inner child is coming forward and unconsciously taking over my sexual relationship with Don; and he is moving into his dominant perpetrator self and not really engaging my adult woman self. This awareness somehow empowers Don to think he can fix our relationship, and he starts to instruct me on how I need to change.

He states, "You need to be able to express your feelings, identify your needs and ask for what you want. You do want to have a conscious relationship, don't you?"

"Sure, why not?" I say. I start to feel that this idea of conscious relationship is the new ideal that is becoming the justification of his berating me. I go on. "All I know is I just want to be loved for who I am in my journey. Half the time, I do not know how I feel. When we try to talk about important things, I feel like you are interrogating me. I hate it when you act like you are the only one who knows anything."

He glares at me with dark eyes of disgust and puffs his chest as he shouts at me. "Just tell the truth." The tension in the air is growing. My shoulders begin rising up to my ears, and my stomach feels hot. A wave of hatred for Don begins to creep up my spine, lodge in my throat and make my ears burn.

Now I know what I feel. I tell him, "I think you are mean. I hate it when you start asking me questions and then make me feel like shit when I don't give you the answer that you want." There is pure venom in my voice.

He blurts, "You are attacking me. Being truthful means telling me how you are feeling without blaming." Don is backing away from me.

I hate him. I hate him. I hate him. I do not ever say the right thing. Heat is moving upward from my gut, crawling into my chest and then my face reddens. I do not know what to say. I feel trapped. I am walking on eggshells, anticipating a barrage of punishing words to drill down upon me at any moment as he attempts to teach me how I am supposed to be in this relationship. I clam up and refuse to talk about the issues he wants to bring forward. *It will only lead to a fight. What am I doing in this scary relationship? How did this happen?*

I started heavily berating myself. *If I just could just find a way to communicate properly with Don, then he would not be so angry. If I could just heal and become more aware of my feelings, then we could have a good relationship. If I could just feel my own passion for life, then we could figure out a future together and be happy.*

We continually hit a wall of pain and anger that starts dominating our relationship. I am feeling numb all the time, and I can barely identify my needs. I am leaving my body, and Don is so angry and frustrated because he feels unsafe when I go numb.

I kept trying to make the relationship work. I sought out Robin and Joseph so I could understand why so much pain was being triggered by Don. Don sometimes joined the sessions, as well. I would meet the child part of me that kept coming forward in my relationship with Don and repair her, so she would not engage in sex with Don. I connected with her so she could let me love her and help her feel safe. I realized I was playing out my relationship with my father with Don. I was anticipating Don abusing me and sure enough he did. I did not feel wanted or accepted for where I was really at in my life, and I was trying to perform and be the good girl.

Robin and Joseph gave us exercises to try when we were triggered. We were instructed to slow down our breath, to track the sensations of our body, to go inside and pull back the projections and the blame, and to connect with what we really felt in the moment. We were given strategies to help us through our conflicts, but most of the time Don was not willing to use them. I am not feeling safe at all in this relationship. I move into the extra bedroom, and we still try to get through our painful triggers and have some sort of companionship. We often eat meals together, soak in the hot tub, and walk the dog. We are making an effort.

When the tension was high, Don would say, "I'm going fishing." It was as if he was pulling my heart out of my chest; I felt so abandoned. He was angry and spiteful, taking his whole self with him. *What is the matter with me?* I cried and cried.

One evening we bicycle out into the dark night with our headlamps on to exercise Don's dog. "Hey look, I have a bell on my bike." Don is showing off his latest gadget.

135

I turn my head to look. "Very cool." The tires of my bike are moving from the compact dirt road into the sandy shoulder. My arms tense to try and steer the tires back on course. As I twist the handles of my bicycle, I topple toward my right and slam into the ground. Pain is shooting up my right leg. As I lay there, I feel myself leaving my body as I had been programmed to do in my childhood. With a flat voice, I look at Don and say, "I think I've broken my leg."

Don gets me to the hospital.

In the Emergency Room, we check in with the triage nurse. "Please rate your level of pain on a scale from one to ten."

I say, calmly, "It's a six or so." She is shocked. I am not in my body and do not feel.

I go home from the ER in a cast, helpless and dependent on Don. He takes over. I will need surgery as soon as the swelling goes down. He takes care of everything, food, movie rentals, doctor appointments and phone calls. Soon we discover from the surgeon that my leg should have had a more substantial cast than what I received in the ER. Fortunately, no permanent damage was done, and the surgeon brilliantly repairs my leg. Don tells me that he has consulted his lawyer friend about suing the ER for an inadequate cast. "What?" I shout. "You haven't even asked me what *I* want to do, and you've already talked to a lawyer?" Heat is surging through my chest as my nostrils flare. I can barely contain my hatred. My hatred is bigger than my love.

MAKING SENSE OF THE MAYHEM

In the fall of 2009, I dissolve our intimate relationship and move into my own place. I now know that if I have an intimate partner, it must be someone who wants to be there for me and is committed to the journey. Don never fully chose me or committed to creating a partnership. As painful as the relationship with Don was, I learned so much about myself. Now I know that I was trying to wake myself up. This was a necessary step in my developing awareness. After a counseling session with Robin and Joseph, I realize that love and intimacy is going to bring up the hatred in my body from past abuse. The love and intimacy that I started feeling with Don had activated my real hatred toward men from my childhood abuse. I was starting to consider that my hatred was stored in the parts of my body that were wounded, my vagina, my anus, all the erotic parts.

Robin and Joseph are available to take me on this next step of healing. Robin tells me, "In the soul work that we do of understanding how Don is part of your soul's evolution and learning, we need to ask what really attracted you to Don. Do you have similar perpetrator energy as he does? We know you have had sexual trauma, so perhaps you were playing the victim to his victimizer. What was he showing you inside yourself? What quality of being did he represent in you? What are your beliefs about intimacy and sex? In other words, who is Don in you?" As painful as looking at myself this way is, I do not want to be part of another traumatic relationship. I am ready to find out.

I am in a session. As I breathe deeply and send my breath into my body, I sink down into myself. I feel deeply in my heart my desire to heal the part of me that Don has been showing me. Through prayer we invoke that part of my soul. I feel its presence coming closer to me. In my mind's eye, I see an image of a scaly reptile with a tail. We begin to dialog with this part to try to understand what it is. With Robin's coaching, I talk to this part.

I ask, "What is your purpose?" *I see scales. How can that possibly be me?*

This part responds, "I want to control everyone and everything."

I ask, "Why? Where did you come from?"

It responds, "It is just my way. I am attached to humans who want to kill. I'm unlovable and nobody would ever freely give me love so I have to just take it."

I say, "So, you want love."

It says, "I have done bad things and I hate myself. I don't deserve love."

I ask, "Do you know that you do not have to earn love?"

It says, "But I have done terrible things."

I say, "Love is for everyone. You do not have to control anything to 'get' love. You are lovable just because you exist. Did you know that?"

It replies. "No. I was told that wanting love meant I was weak. I have to be strong."

I tell it, "You didn't know any better. Can you have compassion for yourself because you didn't know about love?"

It says, "I guess so."

I say, "I am choosing to love and forgive you because you didn't know about love. Taking what we want creates more harm. Power over others hurts my life, and then I attract it from others. Can you forgive yourself for what you did when you didn't know you were lovable?"

It says, "I want to. It will take time. I did not know I could just have love without taking from someone else. It will take a little time to get used to this idea."

I realize I am educating the reptilian part of my soul that believes it is a monster and never worthy of love. And by embracing this part of me, it starts to change its behavior in me.

I come to understand that there are spirit forms that have attached to parts of my soul. Robin shares with me that these reptilian entities are often attracted to satanic abuse survivors and perpetrators. They actually are behind much of the abuse, and they are interdimensional and do not always show up in physical form. We experience them through the feeling body and intuition and some psychics can see them. Much of the imagery of the devil from ancient times duplicate the reptilian features. As I talk to this reptilian form inside my soul stream, I realize it is a masculine part, and that the masculine part of me sees itself as a monster. My inner child parts have been terrified of this other male part of me. I feel some child parts inside of me relaxing as I reeducate him to surrender into my heart and give up his victimizer role in my soul and in me.

After practicing dialoging with this part of me for several weeks, I ask it, "What do you believe about yourself now?"

The reply is, "I actually belong to you and do deserve love. I just had not believed that before. I did not think I could be forgiven. I am glad I am not isolated from healing anymore."

From my heart I respond, "If I can help you heal, we don't have to attract abuse anymore. Your self-hatred and self-judgment have attracted abuse in my life. I would like to be done with that cycle."

TWISTED SEXUALITY

It is January 2010, a few months after I have left Don, when I ask myself what my next steps of healing are. I had become keenly aware that my sexual erogenous zones were carrying a multitude of pain, pleasure, violent memories, hatred, and a plethora of confusion. I decide that I am ready to address this situation. I pick Robin and Ahara to guide me in this work because I feel safe with them. Ahara is a body work specialist who frequently works with trauma survivors. She is masterful with feeling and sensing the energies that are in the human body and helping create awareness about the consciousness that resides there. She has the expertise to help me release trauma and emotions in my body tissue and muscles. As I approach them with my request, I know that the most terrifying area for me is everything below my belly button. I know now, after being with Don, that this is where my terror is held. Together they can help me explore what is in my lower body. They respect my boundaries, and body work has now become a powerful tool for my healing.

I am asking them to touch me in areas that are highly charged so that I can practice guiding them slowly to do energy work in these painful places. I have discovered that when I express with sound and movement, the pain releases and resolves. We create a safe environment for this work. Robin accesses her spiritual guidance so she can amplify her sensitivity to see where my body is holding the blockages of my trauma. We slow the pace down, and then I invite Ahara to place her hand on my inner thigh. I gently start to breathe into this area. I am looking into her eyes. They are gentle. But I start tensing up. I feel disconnected from myself. I focus intently on my breath and remind myself of my desire to heal. Soon my brave face is dissolving, giving way to terror. I open my mouth and gulp in some air to support the loud sound that wants to come forth. Even though Ahara is inviting me to express, I do not seem able to allow the energy to move. Even though I know how to breathe through emotional pain, I get stuck.

I say, "You must be triggering a memory, Ahara. I feel scared. I want to freeze and shut down. I can't connect and move the energy like I have before." We, as a team, decide to stop and to build more safety and stronger, loving resource in my body before working like this again.

The next day I am pacing in my house. I am highly irritable and cannot relax. Robin decides to come by to check on me. It is a gray, cold day and a layer of snow disguises the thick sheet of ice that covers the roads. *Why the heck isn't she here?* My anger and impatience are mounting. *I will go get my mail while I wait for her.* As I sit down to put on my snow boots, I say to myself, *I do not want to slip so I am going to put on my rubber-soled boots.* I walk outside and whoosh, down I go. *Ouch! Damn. My wrist looks like a bent fork.* With pain shooting up my arm, I crawl to my door in silence, carefully thrusting myself forward with my left arm, dragging my body over the threshold. I make it into my house and wait for Robin. It has been ten months since I broke my leg. *Another break! I cannot believe it.*

My wrist was broken into many pieces. I needed surgery again. I intuitively knew that some part of me was hijacking my memories and my healing process. Robin, Joseph, Ahara and I agree that we need to pause and understand how my breaks are connected to a subconscious aspect to stop me from uncovering more memories. I realized that something similar had happened in 2003. During a time where I was uncovering a highly guarded memory, I had experienced an impulse, absent of thought, to step out into oncoming traffic, but at the last second, caught myself. Besides my depression and suicidal thoughts, this latest incident of breaking my arm showed me that I was moving into dangerous territory of memory. Dawn and I acknowledged that we were bumping up against important secrets. The more committed I became to go into my body and look at what really happened to me, the more my terror of telling the truth increased.

THE PROCESS OF DEPROGRAMMING

Robin, Joseph, and Ahara committed to understanding how I was unconsciously programmed to get hurt or have suicidal ideation when I got close to my memories. I noticed that as I made a stronger commitment to know what happened to me, the healing processes we did uncoupled the mind control that gave me the impulse to kill myself or hurt myself when I was close to my memories. We understood these programmed thoughts and impulses were designed to sabotage my whistleblowing to stop satanic abuse. This is why so many people are so disempowered to tell the truth about ritual abuse. They have suicide programming. Robin, Joseph, and Ahara resolved that they would learn how to deprogram the impulse for suicide before helping me access any more memories. My healing team was committing to make my process safe for me.

I began investigating the topic of SRA and programmed self-harm and found there was a link between SRA and CIA mind control programming to create military assassins. The accidents suggested that I was not just a victim of satanic rituals but that there was something even more insidious and purposeful in my programming.

I am sitting in the healing room with Robin. We are getting ready to begin a session. I hear a cell phone ringing, and it is in my purse. I open my purse to retrieve the ringing phone and notice it is not my phone. I freeze. *How in hell did that phone get into my purse?* I can't think. I am in shock. "Where did this phone come from?" I blurt out to Robin.

"Aren't you going to answer it?" she asks.

"It's not mine," I say. For a split second I fear that I am crazy, and that some part of me knows some clandestine secret about this phone. I look at Robin. Her presence is grounding me bringing me back to the here and now. I decide to answer it.

"Hello," I squeak out.

"This is John. I am Nancy's husband. She lost her phone in exercise class this morning. Who is this?"

"Oh. Well, my name is Beth. Somehow this phone got into my purse." My brain is starting to relax, able to take in information. He tells me that during class Nancy had asked her son to put her phone into her purse. He got the wrong purse.

My visceral reaction during this incident showed me my level of terror about things unremembered. Panic had surged through my veins as unconscious and presumed meanings about my life showed me that I deeply feared what I still did not know. I often wondered if I was under psychic surveillance from some source. I had heard about remote viewers who could see psychically into other people's spaces. My mind often questioned who I could trust. I was often paranoid. *Am I still being manipulated, and I do not know it? What horrific acts have I been programmed to participate in that I do not remember?* Dawn, too, was fearful that she had caused a lot more harm to others than she had recalled. We had to commit to compassion for ourselves as trained, programmed children in order to deconstruct the programming. Without love, none of this would heal.

Robin, Joseph, Ahara, Dawn, and I worked consistently and simultaneously to deeply explore the nature of suicidal programming and self-punishing accidents. We discovered that the more access that Dawn and I gained to facts of who, what, and where, the more symptoms revealed themselves in many forms. Thoughts of suicide, paranoia feelings, a desire to stop the healing work, impulses to isolate, and feelings of deep hopelessness emerged. We went collectively to the spiritual realms to ask for guidance on how to deconstruct these impulses in both Dawn and me. Through energy work, anchored in love, Dawn and I were able to receive safety back in our bodies and deconstruct the suicide and self-punishing impulses in our alternate personalities and soul parts. We started feeling safer than ever before, and my commitment to telling the truth about my journey began to rise. I wanted to tell the truth that could expose how so many people are being manipulated by elite perpetrators. I was not alone in my experience. This is how assassins are trained to kill with no memory of it. I realized that before I broke my wrist,

I had enrolled in a class to prepare me to tell my story in public. I wanted to be a whistleblower and the saboteur in me stopped it.

I see now that the two breaks of my bones literally cracked open the consciousness of my programming. I have come to understand how I was compartmentalized and trained to be numb. My physical body had faithfully led me to an understanding of some of the workings of my subconscious self. It was a gift in service to my greater awareness of the forces that were programmed to control my life. My soul had committed to healing with me and these painful breaks became a gift.

Without the opportunity for deprogramming, I was not safe enough to go further into the healing work. It was a huge step of learning for the healing team, as well as for Dawn and me. We had now moved into a whole other arena of needing to be safe enough to remember these situations. My greatest commitment was self-love, and I was not willing to risk dying for my healing work. I was not willing to be a martyr. I was grateful to be growing in self-knowledge and awareness. I was starting to see a bigger picture of a whole system of abuse. After all, my father had been employed on a military base.

CHAPTER FIFTEEN

Can I Connect Sex with Love?

I n Spring 2011, I finally felt ready to explore my sexual blocks again. By then I understood that I have to stay present in my body with touch, and body work must happen in a very conscious way. I had heard about tantric yoga as a mode for sexual healing. Robin explained, "Tantra is a sacred spiritual practice that uses the breath to move sexual energy up through the energy centers of the body. As you breathe into the chakras, you can release the energy of old wounds and open the body to pleasure. The pleasure sensations become the healer with kindness and love. I have seen this ancient practice help people heal their sexual wounds."

By this time, I can access my body's feelings, and I want to work with a man. I do not have an intimate partner, so I decide to hire a professional tantra therapist because I want somebody who is conscious and aware. *This will be so weird to pay someone to touch me in an intimate way.* As I am discussing the possibility of working with a professional tantra therapist with Robin, my belly constricts. I say, "I want to do this, but you need to be there with me."

We discuss what my goals are. "I want to practice how to communicate my needs to another about how I would like to be touched. I never realized that I have choices about this. It never crossed my mind before now."

"This will be a huge empowerment step for you, Beth." Robin's voice is encouraging.

Robin talks with the tantra specialist and makes agreements of how to collaborate with him in supporting me. The three of us meet ahead of time to discuss my needs for healing. In my first tantra session, James is standing in the doorway and says, "Welcome. I have prepared this sacred space for you." Rose petals are scattered on the bed where beautiful scarves are draped. The room is warm, and my eyes soften as I gaze upon the beauty. Incense is wafting, several candles are lit, and relaxing music is playing.

I have never been treated with such consideration before. Wow! I feel honored. I am curious, nervous, and shaking as I walk in. "Thank you," I whisper.

Robin then reminds me about the intentions with which this space has been created. "This is a safe container to allow you to experience the first step of pleasure without punishment. The goal is to allow sexual touch for your adult woman self, and your children are to be contained in your heart, not participating in your sexuality." I momentarily check inside and make sure my child selves are tucked away safely in my heart.

James continues setting boundaries. "These are the rules. No kissing, no intercourse. Please express your feelings and needs. You are in charge of your body. I am here to give you pleasurable touch. You may simply receive and enjoy. Just to let you know, I am in a monogamous, committed relationship." I lie down on the bed, noticing the silky feel of the scarf that is wrapped around my torso.

"Ask for what you want, Beth," Robin coaches. I notice that I do not want to look at James' face. Shame wafts over me. I am embarrassed to expose my body. *I will just keep my eyes closed and not look at James.* The massage and warm oil begin to relax me. I let the good touch seep in deeper and deeper as I consciously breathe and open to sensations of pleasure. I have made an agreement in this session to stop the touch at any moment that I am triggered, so that I can then become aware of how to breathe through my feelings in present time. The goal is to breathe through my fear and discomfort without stopping the pleasure, and to allow a new imprint that I am safe being touched when I am in choice.

The first session was a breakthrough for me, as I opened to receive pleasure. What a paradigm shift for me about touch! I enjoyed it, could receive it, and did not leave my body.

Robin's presence added to my sense of safety. The next big risk was to do a session alone with James and practice communicating what I needed to say to feel safe. Empowerment with a man, through my voice, was a skill I needed if I ever was going to be intimate with a lover. James was a safe person to practice this with. Robin would be in a room close by, in case I needed her.

AN UNEXPECTED GIFT

In this solo session, I agree with James that I am trying to keep my eyes open and practice being fully present and not escape any uncomfortable feelings by closing my eyes. I notice before the session I am actually feeling joy about having another pleasurable experience. I have more joy than fear. For the first twenty minutes I am receiving pleasurable relaxation from the massage. Suddenly, a wave of irritation and tension arises. *I do not like what he is doing.* My chest and throat constrict, and I cannot find my voice. I start to close down, and I become mute. My pleasure vanishes.

"I'm angry," I finally mutter. "Please call Robin in."

"What's going on?" she asks.

"I am really frustrated and angry. I am not enjoying this massage. I am shutting down." Emotions are coursing through me, and I want to jump up and run. My rage is up.

Robin asks, "What are you sensing? Is this familiar?"

"I am so angry, and I want to punch someone," I say.

"It feels like you have switched out of your present time self," Robin acknowledges.

"I've enjoyed massage before, but I can't get back to the relaxed pleasure. I am really mad. Why did this have to happen, Robin?"

She responds, "I think, Beth, this is a new part of yourself."

I take a breath. "This just felt like a change of mood due to my displeasure with the massage. I wonder if this ever happened before and I didn't know it?"

My energy had switched. I had completely shut down all the pleasure, and I became angry, went up into my head and felt very irritable. I could not get back to present time. This was a spontaneous emergence of a split part. Through counseling with Robin, I began to understand that certain sexual experiences would trigger an alternate personality to come forward. This particular personality was only accessible through sexual arousal and was not interested in love and pleasure through touch. Clearly, this alter had been created through sexual violation.

The next step of sexual healing was to integrate my alter's experience so I could move through the programming that sex is unsafe and only linked to violence. This began a process of healing the physical pain in my sexual centers as well as the psychic split that occurred during sexual trauma as a child. This happened throughout many healing sessions with loving touch from Ahara and my own touch.

SEEKING MORE HELP

In the last eight years, I had gone from complete denial of my sexual and ritual abuse to not only uncovering the depths of SRA but the level of mind control and fracturing that I had been functioning with my whole life. I had begun to repair my relationship with my sister where we were actually inspiring each other to keep going deeper into memories because we piggy backed on the material discovered in each other's sessions. I had been sharing with my birth children that there was a strong possibility that they had been involved somehow in satanic rituals even though I had not had mental recall. I had gotten safe enough in my body to stay consciously present during sexual, pleasurable massage, a huge achievement. I had so much to be grateful for beyond anything I could have predicted, and yet I could still feel that I was not free to experience love and sexuality together in my body. The emergence of an alter during my tantric healing session with James had made it clear that I needed to continue healing my sexuality.

Robin and Joseph often asked for extra spiritual guidance in areas that they did not have personal experience. When I approached Robin and Joseph with my desire to link my sexuality with love, Robin's intuition guided her to ask for support from a group of beings that were specifically committed to helping people with severe fracturing and soul splintering. She worked with multidimensional beings who called themselves the Rainbow Unity Beings. They had introduced themselves to Robin and Joseph with several clients who had a desire to repair the soul/body split.

We began a session working with the Rainbow Unity Beings. They asked me a question through Robin. "Are you willing to understand the depths of how your soul has been manipulated? Because you have a belief that if you see your soul, you will go crazy."

In response, I willingly make a commitment that I will listen, feel, and integrate what I can in a healthy, loving way, setting my intention to integrate what my soul needs to show me.

The Beings direct Joseph to place his two hands on my head. He puts one on the back of my head and one on the crown, to bring healing energy to my brain, specifically the pineal area and the hypothalamus. There are crystalline structures in these areas to keep me from my soul memory.

So, I set intention that I want to meet the part of my soul that wants to heal this issue of satanic ritual abuse. The Beings say to me, "We want you to feel the seed of your original galactic tribe. Your tribe is waiting for you to remember who you are."

Through the energy work of Joseph and the Beings that guide Robin, I begin to feel a larger soul-purpose, realizing that I have come to this earth to heal with the law of forgiveness. To stop the violence in my life, I had to meet the parts of my soul that were violent and bring them to love. I began to learn that certain galactic energies had affected the human violence on the earth. When we started worshipping gods outside of ourselves, deities, we began to give our power away and forgot that our essential nature is love. A lot of the reptilian spirit forms provoke dynamics of using force and control of one group of people over another. They actually thrive off of violence. If we feel unlovable as souls, we are vulnerable to these dark forces. It was my job as a soul to come to earth and repair with compassion, the violence, self-judgment, self-hatred and self-condemnation in my soul and body.

THE RAINBOW UNITY BEINGS EXPLAIN HOW MANIPULATING SEXUAL ENERGY AFFECTS SOUL EVOLUTION

In a session where the Rainbow Unity Beings came to assist my healing process, I found the following information so important to my understanding of global human suffering; it supported me to have compassion for myself and so many others, even those who perpetrated against me.

"You have not been willing to understand the gift of your feeling, sensing body to your full remembrance of your soul experiences. If humanity can forget that they are essentially eternal souls, then they can be manipulated through the fear of death. How do the controllers keep humans as sheep? The controllers programmed humanity to deny the sensing body. It is taught to your culture that to feel fears is weak. **If you want to stop humanity from evolving in their soul awareness, disconnect the mind from the heart.** The sexual energies that come forward in your pleasure centers awaken the cellular memory of your higher body if they are connected with your higher soul body.

"As the kundalini awakens in our lower chakras and moves up into our crown, this opens our awareness to our multidimensional nature, our eternal soul. So, these programmed efforts have been very strong in those who have strong spiritual destinies. This includes you, Beth. The stronger the desire to serve humanity, the more effort was made to suppress your sexual healing, freedom, and expression. The stronger your spiritual commitment to serve global healing, the stronger the suppression you attracted of your sexual freedom. Your shame, the judgments, and the programming of shutting down your sexual healing powers has been strong. Just understand, when the kundalini awakens, the gifts of your spiritual centers will be awakened. Each

151

chakra will open. Your freedom to love and be loved will be regained. Your sense of safety in your cellular structure will be maintained and sustained no matter what the circumstances. You need to explore your sexuality in a safe way to learn how your kundalini energies move and how to use them in every organ of your body to rejuvenate and regenerate, especially for your empowerment of your soul destiny. For you to avoid sexual experiences, expression, or pleasure is the decline of your life force. So, your attempt, Beth, to awaken this area is literally your doorway to life. The healing of the first and second chakras is critical to your full awakening."

The Rainbow Unity Beings activated a deep knowing in my heart to reengage my desire for awakening and freedom. They confirmed the complex nature of my programming which demonstrated how I had been damaged and rearranged. They validated that my birth father was programmed to damage me so that I could not trust emotional bonding with pleasure. And, of course, this would affect all my attempts to relate intimately with men. Their words really underscored just how impossible having a loving, sexual relationship had been for me. They continued, "So, to prepare yourself to not have harm and violation, you did not emotionally bond with any other lovers. And when you did, then you could not be sexual. So, the obstacles in your sexual relationship came when you began to really love someone. In your programming, to bond emotionally meant to be violated."

This understanding helped me feel more compassion for the rocky road of relationships with men that I had experienced. I learned that the spiritual mind control that I experienced through satanic ritual was guided by a race line that looked reptilian. This was all much bigger than me.

When Joseph did energy work on my brain, I experienced high frequencies running through my body and restructuring my energy field. I could feel my nervous system healing with the energy work. After receiving these sessions, I realized I could open and allow the memories to flow, and they would not cause fragmentation or mental illness. I was no longer afraid of mental illness and now my capacity to move between the worlds and develop safety was increased. I now had more freedom to bond emotionally and connect sexuality with love.

In the overall larger picture, I started noticing in humanity how sexual distortions exist in every religion. Shame surrounds sexuality which leads to abuse. So many people are manipulated not to feel sexually free and able to bond in loving relationships. **Casting out sexual energies into the underground makes us vulnerable to being manipulated and controlled by others because we no longer have access to our life force. These religious hierarchical systems create human slavery.**

After this session with the Rainbow Unity Beings, I experienced a couple more tantric sessions with James. I acknowledged my body and appreciated how it had chosen to survive. I was able to weep with my body, knowing that I had survived all the torture, and I felt deep compassion for what my body had endured.

CHAPTER SIXTEEN

A Bond Restored

Dawn and I had come a long way in our efforts to heal old wounds and become true friends. And yet hints of these wounds were still popping up consistently.

"What do you think, Beth?" Dawn is waiting for my answer, her clipped tone brings me back to the present. She and my niece are waiting to hear my answer.

"What were you talking about?" I ask. My mind is miles away, and I am drowning in feelings of overwhelm, not sure what the conversation has been about. My stomach lurches and I steel myself for her barrage of criticisms.

"Geez, Beth, what is the matter with you?" Dawn lets out a sigh of exasperation. "Why don't you ever listen?"

My body is shrinking as I withdraw into a tighter space. "I can't stand to be around you when you are so irritable and taking it out on me," I say. I am embarrassed not to have been tracking the conversation. My shoulders cringe, and my heart withdraws, building a wall meant to shut out the shame, but the result is that I shut out Dawn. I lash out. "Not everybody can be a know-it-all encyclopedia like you," I say.

"Well, at least I have *something* to say," she responds.

My breath becomes shallow. I feel a rush of hot arrows moving in my mouth and throat; my closed fists are knotted up, hanging on either side of my body.

These patterns of relating are so painful because I long for more closeness with Dawn. I am triggered by her almost every time we speak. *Geez, how many more layers of pain are there? This seems endless.* But I want something more in our relationship, so I need to keep going. I finally gather my courage and make a request. "Would you be willing to do some work with Robin and Joseph so we can heal this animosity between us?"

"Yes. I get so impatient with you. I don't really want to treat you that way." Dawn's response gave me hope. If I could heal my relationship with my sister, it would create a new foundation for relating to others as well.

Thus, it was in the second decade of the new millennium when we began our dedicated work. We entered into a mutual Intensive for four days where we did both individual and mutual sessions, supported by Robin, Joseph, and Ahara. In a shared session, a memory of our past dynamics emerged. In my mind's eye my emotions paint a picture of the following scenario.

Dawn and I are together. "Keep those children quiet or else!" *someone commands. Fear spikes through my little body and I start to shriek and cry. I have no control over the sounds emerging from my lungs.*

"Get your sister into the water, now Dawn! You know how to silence her. Push her down. Shut her up."

I feel pressure on my head. The shock of the icy water slaps me as I go under. I hold my breath but eventually there is no more air. Everything goes black, and I go limp. Sometime later, I find myself shivering, lying on the ground. I am dazed and confused.

Ahara and Robin help us to come back to present time with somatic tracking, breathing and eye contact. We coach our inner children back into our hearts. I immediately start connecting my refusal to put my head under water with this memory. *I thought I just did not like getting my hair wet. There is more to it than that.*

"I don't know if I can ever feel completely safe in water." I announce.

"Well, that can be repaired," Ahara says.

We devised a plan to work through my water trauma with Dawn and repair our relationship, not only with each other but with water itself.

"How do we do that?" I ask. *I do not think that is going to happen.* My body tenses just thinking about being in water.

"Being in water in a loving, safe way will allow your children to know that they can be safe there," Ahara responds.

We commit to do a session in water that would support me to repair with Dawn. Ahara is an aquatic body-work practitioner in addition to being trained as a trauma specialist and will work with us to support and repair full soul/body healing. So, Robin and Ahara take Dawn and me to a four-foot deep warm water pool where our visceral body memories can be keenly activated. Her expertise in the water is definitely needed here.

"I took swimming lessons and finally got over my fear of being in a pool, but as I step into this water, I feel scared all over again," Dawn says with a quiver in her voice.

The gentle waves are slapping against the side of the pool and push against my body increasing my nausea. "I feel sick to my stomach," I say. "I hope I don't throw up in the pool." *I hate being in this water. Why can't we just do this in a regular session?*

I am sixty, and Dawn is sixty-two, but now a terrified four-year-old child and defiant, confused six-year old are present.

Ahara: Track your nausea, Beth. Breathe into your sensations. Where do you feel them? Do they have a color?

Four-Year-Old Beth: They are in my stomach and are gray and roundish at the edges.

Ahara: Keep breathing into them, Beth. What else do you notice?

Four-Year-Old Beth: They keep changing size. First, they are small, and then they get bigger. Then they go back to being small. [After a few minutes of describing the sensations, Ahara turns her attention to Dawn.]

Ahara: What is happening to you, Dawn? What do you feel in your body?

Six-Year Old Dawn: I feel my legs wanting to kick. [Dawn is wrapping her arms around her body in a firm grasp.]

Ahara: Release your arms and let your arms and legs move in the water. Give yourself permission to move any way you want to move.

Robin: [Dawn and I are standing facing each other.] Beth, is there something you want to tell Dawn?

Four-Year Old Beth: Dawn, I am scared of you in this water. [I look into Dawn's eyes.] I am 'fraid of you. [An intense fear is lodged in my chest, my arms, and my legs. I am aware of the queasiness in my stomach. I start pumping my legs up and down and begin shouting.] No. No. No. I do not want to be in the water.

Robin: We are going to create a safe place for your children with your Governing Center helping them in present time to do what you could not do as children. We can empower your children to bring their own will into this present time with your adult self. Dawn, Beth, do you feel ready to start moving toward the experience physically and reenact the instruction to push Beth down but instead lift Beth out? How does that feel?

Six-Year Old with Adult Dawn: Yes, I want to do that.

Four-Year Old with Adult Beth: Yes, that sounds good. [I adjust my nose plugs and point my head downward, ready to meet the water.] This time I am going under, but I will push back and get help.

[I feel my determination to heal this trauma as the warm water envelops me and I go under. I can feel my feet on the bottom of the four-foot pool. My legs start pushing on the floor of the pool, and I let myself flail. Then I feel Dawn's hands underneath my armpit. I wrap my arms around Dawn, and I feel the water's flow against my skin. I am moving upwards. My head bursts through the surface of the water and I breathe out a long, deep sigh. I begin to cry, feeling warmth slowly enveloping my heart. I hear Dawn's little six-year old voice coming through her adult body.]

Six-Year Old with Adult Dawn: I never wanted to hurt you, Beth. I never wanted to hurt you. They made me do it.

Four-Year Old Beth: I just wanted to be friends with you and play with you.

Six-Year Old with Adult Dawn: But now we are safe, Beth. We are really safe. They cannot hurt us anymore.

[We hug each other for a long time, consciously aware that the mutual pain between us is disappearing in the light of understanding, compassion, and love. Robin and Ahara wrap their arms around us. When I look in their eyes, I see tears.]

Robin: What did you wish you could say to the controllers at that time?

Four-Year Old Beth: I hate you. Why are you so mean to little kids? [Tears are flowing as I express my anger and hatred. Robin coaches me to kick and punch in the water.]

Robin: Dawn, what would you like to say to the controllers?

Six-Year Old Dawn: You cannot make me hurt Beth and other kids anymore. You are not in charge of me. We are sisters, and we love each other.

Four-Year Old Beth: Yeah, we are sisters and we love each other! You cannot stop us from that.

[A surge of power came back to me as Dawn and I voiced our true feelings to our torturers about loving each other. I felt strong and free.]

That evening, our little girl selves wanted to have some fun together. We got out the hot chocolate and cookies and sat down at the table to make paper dolls. I giggled, thinking about how I had really loved paper dolls as a child. "Look at the dress I made for my paper doll," I said to Dawn.

"My paper doll looks like me," she responded. Indeed, Dawn had put her hair into ponytails after being in the water, and her creation looked like a small child, ponytails, and all. I noticed a softening on Dawn's face that I had never seen before. My heart opened even wider. *I can see us spending more time together.*

During our Intensive we became more aware of the ways we were set up to mistrust and betray one another. Trickery was a consistent tactic of our perpetrators. One night I was led to believe that *I* had killed Dawn. And then, there she was the next morning. I never knew what was true and what was not. Now, with these new imprints, seeds of new possibilities for relating were germinating.

"Dawn, I thought I would never feel close to you and be able to trust you completely, but I feel differently now. I am so glad we can finally have fun hanging out. I love you." We pulled each other close, sobbing and hugging one another for a long time. "I don't need to push you away now. That feels so good." I look at Dawn. There is a look of peace on her face. I no longer have to shut her out.

CHAPTER SEVENTEEN

What Have My Alters Done?

By 2012 I finally understood that I had several alters operating in my psyche. According to www.healthyplace.com, "Alters are often considered the multiple personality states being present in one with dissociative identity disorder (DID DSM-5 criteria). These personality states must each have their own enduring pattern of perceiving, relating to and thinking about the environment and self. Alters involve marked discontinuity in sense of self and sense of agency, accompanied by related changes in affect, behavior, consciousness, memory, perception, cognition, and/ or sensory-motor functioning." Missing time is one of the features of Dissociative Identity Disorder.

After my realizations during the tantra work, I now had an understanding with my sister that our ritual abuse created alternate personalities in both of us. We both have lost time, often drawing a blank when questioned about events in the past. This is why I have not been able to consciously remember my abuse. The abuse memories have been held in my body memory, physically, and in my fractured parts. I experience terror and anxiety without clear, direct mental pictures, although I had flashbacks, dreams, and wafts of images throughout my whole life that I had disregarded. I know something happened, but I do not know what. This realization further reminds me of an event from years before where I was deeply puzzled about an incident with a co-worker. In 2005 an incident was reported to me, and I had no idea that this was a sign of an alter stepping forward. I know now that I was programmed to dismiss any feedback that would help me remember what I had done. I was working in a gift shop when the manager pulled me aside. "Beth, Candice is really upset with you. She says that you sharply questioned her when she was taking out some boxes the other day. She thinks you were accusing her of stealing when you asked her to open up the boxes so you could look inside." I scanned my memory, but I could not remember a confrontation with Candice regarding boxes. *What on earth is she talking about?* At the time I had no idea what had happened, and I quickly dismissed the incident from my mind. Now I understand.

MY COMMITMENT TO HEAL MY UNCONSCIOUS PERPETRATOR

In 2004, when the first information of abusing my own children surfaced through my body in horrific guilt and shame, I was not able to recognize the depth of my perpetration with my children. Sometime later, this recognition surfaced, and I felt nauseous and body memories created tingling from my inner thighs up to my vagina. I had to look at this slowly, tracking my body sensations for the truth. I had had many layers of denial protecting me because initially I did not have enough positive resources and self-love to fully face the extent of what I had done without killing myself. **But I knew I had to go on, because if I could not see the truth, I could not help my children heal, and I could not get free.** I had to push forward.

So, at that time the sense of responsibility to repair my psyche, soul and being was driven by a desire to help my children. I look at them as adults, and I understand why they have the challenges they have. I feel compelled to share what I have uncovered with them. But how on earth do I bring this information to them when they do not remember? They are in denial, and maybe sharing my truth can wake them up. But perhaps their denial has kept them sane. Do I dare push them or should I remain silent? If I share too much, is it going to trigger them into a place they are not ready to go? What I do know for sure is that *I* have to repair the splits in me.

During the writing of this book, my alter self came through and told me what I did to Steven. When he was in his bedroom one morning, refusing to get dressed, I was flooded with frustration which brought forth an alter self. I shook and spanked him and left him crying on his bed. Then I left the room and switched back to my kind personality. I walked around the house, returned to his room without any memory of what I had just done. "Come on, Steven, you've got to get your clothes on. Here, I'll help you." I patiently pulled his shirt over his head. I put my arm around him. "There you go, Honey. Good job." My conscious self during Steven's childhood could not understand why he was so angry. Now I do. I can only imagine how crazy making my mothering has been. What a double bind for my children, seeing me kind and pleasant one moment and then acting like a raging maniac the next. Remembering what had taken place with Steven horrified me. I realized that my feelings of rage as a young mother got unleashed with Steven's outbursts of defiance. I used to imagine myself throwing dishes just to hear them shatter. I started processing and concluded that my son Steven was also totally disassociated from his rage, just as I did not know what to do with mine.

By late 2012 my denial was fading, and I began praying for the courage and clarity to face the dreadful deeds that I had enacted on my children. I shed tears of anger, terror, and grief many evenings as I lay in bed and thought about the harm that I had brought to them. No wonder they have struggled with intimacy with others, just as I had with their father. Trusting life was an issue for all of us. I pled into the dark, silent, alone space, hoping for and begging unseen benevolence to touch my life. "Please God, help me see how I have hurt my children. Help me face the truth. Give me the strength to look at this. Please show me how to heal and reveal to me what I need to do. Can there be forgiveness for me? I must find healing for myself and help my children as well."

My session with the Rainbow Unity Beings (Chapter Fifteen) had shown me that I now had the strength to face this lifetime's experiences without completely decompensating into a dysfunctional pile of confusion. I pondered. How do I repair my alters? How do I integrate these parts of myself into wholeness? I went to Robin and Joseph, asking them for assistance in repairing my soul, body, and personality. I also had body work, acupuncture, movement, and art classes in my life to support my overall health.

I am now ready to make a major commitment to heal these aspects of which I have no mental recall.

HEALING THE ALTERS USING SOUL ALCHEMY™

Mind control not only splits personalities but programs the split parts to stay in states of dysfunction and separation from love, such as numbness, passivity, violence, sex slavery, obedience, and so forth. I have discovered this from my own work with the healing team, and the internet research I have done about deprogramming validates this. Svali (2016) writes about the challenges of the healing process because of programming to forget.

The good news is that this programming can be deprogrammed which is what I have been doing all along through the healing work. This engenders hope for me that the deprogramming process through soul work and self-love can bring repair to my alter personalities. I understand that it is part of my soul's spiritual evolution to do this work. I have always known deep inside of me that my soul was co-creating my experiences and that I chose my parents, and my children chose me. The messages from the Rainbow Unity Beings reminded me of the truth that I am an eternal being. This knowledge has helped me evolve my soul. My circumstances have been such that there has been only one path for my healing and that is through the grace of God. As I look back now, I see how I have been divinely guided at many junctures of my life. From the moments of spiritual freedom that I experienced at age ten on my roller skates, to my prayers whispered to the night sky as a teenager, to my instant recognition of Robin when I met her, I have experienced a core connection through which grace has flowed, helping me to find my way. Above all, I had to know that I am a child of God and deserve to heal, no matter what I have done.

During their years of healing work, Robin, Joseph, and Ahara have developed the process of Soul Alchemy™ (see Appendix). It is defined as "…a multidimensional, conscious evolutionary process that creates healing through one's soul, body, and heart partnership. Through this partnership, there is an alchemy that allows for our human personal freedom, joy, internal and external unity. It is a process of choosing wholeness, compassion, and self-love. It is a spiritual philosophy of living that honors all life and each individual's right to their own soul's path. Wholeness is empowered through the equal value between spirit and body. Soul Alchemy™ is grounded in the wisdom that our soul's embodiment is for the purpose of growth and spiritual learning." For me, Soul Alchemy™ encompasses a very grounded process by which I can connect with my present-time self and use somatic tracking skills, energy tools, and prayer and invocation to command my energetic space. Soul Alchemy™ uses soul dialog to consciously retrieve my soul fragments and bring them into wholeness. It is the main way I have retrieved my soul and alters and inner children. These processes allow my soul to become grounded in my body.

The Healing Team has found the principles of Frederick "Fritz" Perls' Gestalt Therapy (Simply Explained, 2017) and Polarity Therapy (Chitty, 2017) to support the process of Soul Retrieval. My work to learn about my alters was done very methodically by utilizing the Chair Dialog Polarity Healing process. Ahara was trained by John Chitty, an expert in polarity healing; she then brought this process to the Sustainable Love Healing Team. This process created a very strong structure that helped us discern the difference between past, present, and future aspects of self. This was needed because the disorganization, chaos and confusion of my unconscious aspects was overwhelming. It helped my consciousness define the missing parts. I was able to discern the difference between present-time self and the alters, present-time self and my inner children, and present-time self and spirit entities that were controlling me. It also helped me discern the difference between my masculine soul parts and feminine soul parts. Soul Alchemy™ calls the present-time self that is connected to the eternal soul's wisdom and the innate body intelligence, the Governing Center.

The Governing Center is the heart intelligence and body awareness that holds the truth of how to heal myself through self-love. I feel it in my physical heart. It is a spiritual and physical power that I believe everyone has. I envision the Governing Center as a rainbow flame emanating from a beautiful, sacred sanctuary that resides in my heart. In this sanctuary burns the eternal flame of my being. This is what the alters integrate into. Robin explains, "The alters have to be witnessed by the core sovereign self. The goal is total integration of all the alters with the ego, unified with love, with the soul. The ego identity, as it bows to the heart, unifies with the soul and with the purpose of self-love." One of the chairs is always for the Governing Center when we are integrating an alter personality.

I would like to share an experience that my healing coach, Ahara, told me about that helped me understand alters. This is what she said. "One afternoon after a session, I came to visit you in your home. I sat next to you on the couch and put my arm around you. As I did that, you turned transparent and I saw you had these little sores on you. I could see little X's on your body that were like little red marks on top of this white, pasty look. The alter was showing itself in your current personality. I knew your core personality was there even though you were transparent. The alter was having an embodied experience for a moment. And your body just glowed. It felt like your whole body was vibrating differently than normal with this added alter. It was like it was getting embodied with you for the first time. You were physical but that part was not physical, and I took a breath. I had you look in my eyes. And then I started talking to you and I said, 'All parts of Beth are welcome here, and you have to be in agreement with Governing Self. All parts have to be in agreement with this body; they can't take it over.'

"For me, Beth, it was a magical moment. It was spontaneous, not part of a healing session. We were not just talking theory. This was tangible, experiential, kinesthetic. This part was coming in because you invited it. I did not see this part as being manipulated by a trigger to come in. You opened your heart and said, 'I want to know you.' It did not know it belonged with you until you invited it in with love.

"This alter wasn't mean. It was pretty vulnerable. It did not experience itself as human, and you were bringing it in to a safe and loving experience. You, from your human love, were bringing this in. It was a repair space and it just needed some holding with appreciation and love. And you did not leave. I just helped you ground. It felt like a necessary part to know that it could be in loving presence with you and me."

Ahara went on to share her perceptions of alters and what she has learned with this work. "We have to call alters back through our being, through our love, not our minds. It has to have that immense, deep, connected knowing for it to come back. So, I think it is a development of heart, of knowing our full self with heart, to actually call parts of ourselves back. When some part has been that hurt and separated, so compartmentalized that it doesn't even know you, recognize you or understand you, you as the conscious self have to recognize that it is you. And you can bring that vibrational frequency from your heart that goes through all time, space, and dimension to bring it home. The heart is the space of knowing oneself as an eternal being, and *that* your alters will recognize.

"It was one of the first times we started really understanding alters. Some alters are programmed to stay separate while the body is being tortured. Some alters are holding all the torture memories. Some alters do not want to know that the body exists because it is so painful. Some alters get manipulated in the astral plane to do things. Sometimes alters have their own evolutionary journey outside of the body in other dimensions and have their own soul evolution, disconnected from conscious self. When you reconnect, it has to learn who you are. You have to learn what it has been through, learn about one another, let it catch up to being human and what has really happened.

"That was at the beginning of finding alters. I do not think we had planned to find that part. It came forward for about forty-five minutes. Then you came back to your present self."

CHAIR DIALOG WITH AN ALTER

In fall of 2016, I was participating in a community training for practitioners where we were learning about Soul Alchemy™ work, when a familiar feeling emerged that was knocking on my consciousness door. My normal strategy of trying to figure this out in my head kicked in. When I shared this feeling with my healing-team-class partner and reflected further on what I knew about myself, I realized it was probably something that I had buried in my unconscious. So, I went in for a one-on-one session, and my Governing Center, my heart, told me to ask about age thirty-two.

As we always do to prepare for dialog with an alter, we placed two chairs across from one another, one for my present-time self speaking from my Governing Center, and one for my young mother self. When I am in Governing Center, I use the Rainbow Light Energy Tool and somatic tools to get totally in my heart and focus in present time before dialoging. In this dialog, my physical body moves back and forth from chair to chair, embodying whoever is speaking. One of the most powerful techniques of getting to the truth of my differing realities is using somatic tracking in my body in whatever chair I am in. I track my sensations, looking for experiences of pressure, warmth, heat, cold, tingles, arrows, pricks, shapes, designs, colors, tightness, openness, tension, relaxation, moisture, dryness, light, heavy, pain, pleasure, and so forth. I allow movement and sound to emerge spontaneously. We avoid using emotional words or mental analysis.

What follows is an example of a session with Robin and Ahara, working with my thirty-two-year old and her alter.

[I take a deep breath and look around the room. I feel the solid connection that my feet have to the floor. I focus on the warmth and caring in my heart for myself, my journey, and all parts of myself. I am in present time.]

Governing Center (GC), coached by Robin: I call forth my Eternal Soul to help me heal. I ask for all my helpers and guides in spirit to come forth. I am ready to face the truth. I am no longer going to judge or shame what I have done. I am here to bring love to this part so I can stop the harmful behavior.

[I ask my thirty-two-year old to come forward. I go to the chair that is for her after I ask this question.]

GC: Are you aware that we were hurt as children? I am now, at sixty-six years old, understanding that we did things that we have no conscious memory of.

Switch chairs. [As I sit in the chair for thirty-two, I start tracking the changed sensations in my body. The underside of my thighs is tingling. My throat is dry. My breathing is shallow.]

Thirty-Two: I am depressed. I feel awful all the time. I do not know why I feel so bad. I do not know how to deal with Steven's tantrums. I get so frustrated.

[To help her understand her depression, I explain to my conscious thirty-two year old about the level of abuse that I have been in, and I educate her extensively about what I have learned about our family's cult abuse and the rituals and share about my healing path.]

GC: There is another part of you that split off that will help you understand your depression and the abuse that you experienced during your life.

Thirty-Two: Okay. I want to meet this part.

GC: All of this can be healed. I want all of me to be home in my heart in present time.

Thirty-Two: Okay.

[We bring in another chair for the Thirty-Two Alter. I invoke the thirty-two part of me that has been forgotten. When I sit in that chair, I am flooded with many sensations. I am in a different aspect of me. My throat tightens, and my voice is changing. My breath becomes shallow. I feel energy rushing through my arms.]

GC: Thank you for coming forward. I am sixty-six years old and coming to you from the future. I am invoking you because you are still connected to me through my soul, but you have become unconscious. I am trying to bring you into conscious awareness that you belong to me. I come to you with deep wisdom and compassion for what happened when you were young. Did you know that I, Beth, and you (thirty-two-alter) were abused as a child?

Switch chairs.

Thirty-Two Alter (TTA): No.

Switch chairs.

GC: We, as a child, had many experiences where we were tortured and then were trained to hurt others. Do you know about that?

Switch chairs.

TTA: No. I only know about what I do.

Switch chairs.

GC: What do you do?

Switch chairs.

TTA: I come out when the telephone rings. Two rings.

Switch chairs.

GC: And then what happens?

Switch chairs.

TTA: I go get Steven and take him into his bedroom. I put him on the bed. I have to follow their instructions.

Switch chairs.

GC: Whose instructions?

Switch chairs.

TTA: I do not know their names. But they tell me that I have to prepare my children for the rituals.

[I am quickly moving back and forth between the chairs as Robin is supporting me. She says, "Just breathe, Beth. Feel the sensations in your body as you take in what was just said." A wave of heat moves through my skin. I get the courage to ask the next question.]

GC: How did you prepare them?

Switch chairs.

TTA: I put objects in their anus. They told me I must widen the opening to make it less painful for Steven during the rituals. 'Your children will thank you' is what they told me.

Switch chairs.

GC: [In present time I gasp.] And did you do this?

Switch chairs.

TTA: Yes, because they said that if I did not do it, they would take over and it would be much worse for my children and me.

Switch chairs.

GC: So, you wanted to make it easier for your children.

Switch chairs.

TTA: Yes. And I had to teach them to be silent. I pushed a rag into Steven's mouth and pinched off his nose.

Switch chairs.

GC: Was that how you taught him to be quiet?

Switch chairs.

TTA: Yes. I would keep him pinched off until I saw his limbs flailing and I could feel him leaving his body. At the last moment, before he was gone for too long, I let go to bring him back to life.

Switch chairs.

GC: You knew when to bring him back?

Switch chairs.

TTA: Yes, I knew.

Switch chairs.

GC: How did you know?

Switch chairs.

TTA: I knew how to leave my body and come back. I would go to the light and forget everything.

Switch chairs.

[I feel deep fear surging through my veins as I receive this information. Robin coaches me to accept these sensations. I am building a foundation of love and compassion for my split parts. My ears are tingling, my face is hot and flushed, as the information comes in. I am stunned and I become nauseated. My current self begins to sob in present time. *My poor babies. I am so sorry. I am so sorry.*]

GC: I, your future self, can feel and see that you did not want to do this. Do you know why you did this? Do you know why this happened?

Switch chairs.

TTA: Because if I did not, they would kill me and my children.

Switch chairs.

GC: So, you were actually trying to save your own life, and you were actually trying to save your children's lives. [Tears are running down my cheeks. I feel dry, parched, like I have not had water for days.]

Switch chairs.

TTA: Yes.

GC: From my own heart at age sixty-six, I send you compassion for your deep confusion. You are a part of me that has been hiding, and they cannot hurt us anymore. Did you know I got away from those people and you belong to me?

Switch chairs.

TTA: I do? I did not know I belonged with you. Can you help me? I do not want to do this ever again.

Switch chairs.

[Robin coaches me, telling me to reassure my parts that we are safe now.]

GC: We are out of the cult now. They cannot hurt us anymore. I have healed so many parts of me that you are safe now to come home and tell the truth. I love you, and I know you did not ever want to be mean. You never wanted to hurt children and I know that.

Switch chairs.

TTA: I want to be with you. I do not want to hurt anyone ever again. How can you love me knowing what I have done?

Switch chairs.

GC: You were trained to do this when you were a little girl, and they split you off from the memory that you were trained to be this way. Until now, you had no way of knowing that you were tortured. You just became the torturer. I love you because you are a part of me, and you deserve love.

GC [With coaching from Robin]: We are going to release the beliefs now that you can never be loved, that you can never be forgiven, and that you always have to hide. Because I am here for you in current time. We can release the compartmentalization that has kept you in denial and separate from me. And I am going to find out when and how you were trained to kill and make sure that we have all the other parts from your childhood that affect you.

Switch chairs.

TTA: I thought I was the only one.

Switch chairs.

GC: No, there are many parts that were trained to kill. You are connected to the children that were split off, too. We are going to bring you all home into my sanctuary and deprogram you from ever having to hurt another again.

The Sustainable Love Healing Team did several processes to support the deconstruction of the belief structures of my programming. My Thirty-Two-Year Old and her alter needed to develop compassion for one another so they could accept each other and heal their split. This is their dialog.

GC: Thirty-Two, how do you feel about this alter?

Thirty-Two: She is pretty nasty. I cannot believe what she did to my children.

GC: Can you understand why she acted that way?

TT: Well, yes. I heard what she had to say about being afraid of being killed. So, I see she did not feel she had any choice.

GC: That is right. She was doing the best she could and trying to save her children. Thirty-Two Alter, how do you feel about Thirty-Two?

TTA: She let me do all the dirty work and pretended to be such an outstanding citizen. She was willing to overlook all of it. She needs to wake up.

GC: Can you understand why she could not face what you had to do?

TTA: Yes. I see that.

GC: Can you forgive each other and appreciate that it took both of you to keep everyone alive?

TTA: Yes, as long as she does not blame me for everything, I can forgive her.

TT: Yes, I really do appreciate how she helped me out. I see how much I needed her.

GC: Can you stand next to one another and join hands so you can come into my heart together, as one?

[I stand up and "see" them joining hands and walk over to my Governing Center. We are now together in my heart.]

I received several bodywork sessions to integrate this memory. Massage provided a stimulus for the emotions to move as I expressed my rage and sorrow day after day. It took about a week and a half before I could feel completely back in present time with Thirty-Two personality and alter integrated and back on board.

As I started integrating alters, my wholeness began to increase. I had more capacity for feeling my body. Looking back now, I see how numb and programmed I had been, acting like a robot. But I was beginning to defrost and the more parts I brought in, the more alive I felt. I felt my outrage and sadness for the violence that had riddled my life. The need and ability to express a normal, human response to my abuse became greater and greater. I was becoming an enlivened, compassionate woman who could feel again. In the evening I now snuggled with my sweet cocker spaniel. Her dark brown eyes often met mine as we gazed with one another. I felt loved by this innocent animal and was delighted to be a mama to this fur baby. Warmth spread throughout my body as my heart opened in amazement and trust.

My work with the team transformed into more role playing which allowed the self-expression that I had been denied. As I got healthier and healthier, I did not lose time anymore.

And I attempted to talk with my children. Soon after, Steven continued in his healing work.

I went through many additional cycles of integrating alters. We discovered that every alter I met was directly connected to a child trauma. One of the core strategies of supporting my alters in becoming human and bringing them to current time was to give them a chance to express what they could not express due to their programming. I could feel energy moving in my body, and I recognized that I was feeling at a level much deeper than ever before. Role playing allowed the alters to say and show what they had never been able to express. Role play creates a context which activates the subconscious, just as dance therapy, psychodrama, and art therapy help unlock the hidden subconscious. These embodied practices of movement are used by Soul Alchemy™ to allow the denied subconscious to come forward.

CHAPTER EIGHTEEN

The Power of My Soul to Co-Create Healing

A ROLE PLAY TO DEPROGRAM AN ALTER

To deprogram the alters, it was necessary to heal the trauma of my child parts that fueled the behavior of my adult. At this point, the healing team and I now understood that the unexpressed emotional rage toward my abusers was used to fuel abuse of others. This is the epitome of emotional manipulation. It was very sophisticated and insidious.

In one of my sessions in 2016, Robin directed a role play to deprogram the ritual experience of my twelve-year old (Chapter Four) that was fueling a lot of my alternate personalities. Another practitioner joined us to help with the role play. As I embodied Twelve in chair work, she spoke to me and said that she was the bride of the Anti-Christ. What follows is a description of the role play that we did with Twelve who was programmed to kill.

Note to the Reader: This material may be very triggering for some readers. Please take your time. As I worked with this material, I had an incredible amount of support so that I could stay in present time as I healed these energies. My intention in sharing this is to show the process of breaking down the programming and reclaiming my will to say no to abuse.

We begin with a dialog with my mother's soul. We spoke to my mother's spirit to understand the circumstances of how this ritual got passed down from her to me and my family. Because chair work can also be used to talk to other people's souls and consciousness, we placed two chairs across from one another, one for my Governing Center and one for my mother's soul. Then we invoked her soul. I winced as I anticipated receiving information that would disgust me and that I could barely listen to, so I slowed down and focused on the love in my heart as I spoke to her soul.

Governing Center (GC): Mom, we are not here to punish or harm. We are here for compassion and understanding. This is a safe place to tell the truth. I do not wish to create karma by attacking you. You were also caught in this ritual. I know now that you were programmed. I want to know about your experience.

Switch chairs.

Mother's Soul: [As I am experiencing my mother's soul, I feel drugged. I am woozy, and it is difficult to keep myself upright.] What do you want to know?

Switch chairs.

GC: Were you in rituals? Were you drugged?

Switch chairs.

Mother's Soul (in a slurred voice): Yes, I was drugged and hypnotized. They made me do it. I wanted you to be the bride of the Anti-Christ. That elevated me to an important position.

Switch chairs.

GC: So, you were willing to sacrifice me for yourself?

Switch chairs.

[As I embody my mother, my hands are clinched, and my fingers are writhing. I feel the excitement in her, anticipating what this will do for her status. Her mouth is twisting, and her breath takes on a hissing sound. The team noticed that there was an entity attached to her. It was not just her soul that we were talking with. It was a separate spiritual force that had taken over my mother. Some see these forces as reptilian, snake, demonic energies.]

Mother's Soul: This ceremony was a great honor, not just for me but for you. I ignored your protests even though I was hurt and insulted that you would be so ungrateful. I knew you would be better off having this power. We were both gaining status and power.

[Immediately my natural anger rises. My personality now, instead of going numb and disassociating, goes into healthy anger.]

GC: Mom, the part of me that felt powerless and a victim
       wanted me to dominate and control, but that is
       not where I am now. I want to understand what
       happened.

My mother's soul vibration was in the space, and all of the
practitioners could feel it and see it psychically, and that
activated even more memory than I had had earlier. I was
able to access more truth in my own body.

GC: Thank you, Mom, for coming. I hope you can heal
       your wounds. You do not have to be stuck anymore.
       I am breaking the contracts to be the Anti-Christ.
       I am not passing this down to the next generation.
       You may leave this room now. I have the information
       that I need.

The practitioners gathered to do a prayer for my mother.
"Great Spirit, Mother/Father God, we thank this soul for
supporting Beth to understand her co-creation, and we ask
this soul to be healed in any way that is in divine right order
for her. We send healing energy, and we ask for the assistance
of anyone who can help [mother's name] move through her
own self-judgment and self-hatred into the next stage of her
healing. We ask for the angels of unity consciousness to help
her. We bless her into that step with grace and ease. We declare
to her mother, you are no longer allowed to manipulate and
control Beth from the spiritual or physical worlds."

My mother passed over to the other side a few months after
this encounter. There is help on the other side for healing.
Thus, she can continue healing on the other side, if she so
chooses.

The next step in the session was the role play to repair my
twelve-year-old child alter by empowering her through my

current time perspective. We explained to her that Gaia, who is a part of Robin, will guide the role play. Robin is not going away, her body is still present along with her personality, and she is letting this part of herself guide us. Another healing practitioner joins us to role play my mother. We set up the room with objects and a table to represent the ritual space that Twelve remembered. Robin and I prepared the practitioner who was playing my mother with information about my mother, her role, and key phrases of what was said to me. She is then sent out of the room. She is told to enter when she hears knocking on the door. A drum beats.

I stand up in my Governing Center to allow my anger, my new-found boundaries, and my outrage to energize me. I take command of the situation by reminding Twelve that I am here, and now we are going to get our power back and stop the abuse.

The practitioners and I held hands and offered this prayer to align with my will to love and move through the emotional content of Twelve who wanted to die. "Mother/Father God, we pray now to our Source and all of our Eternal Soul essences, our Source of Love, to access the holographic reality, expand it so we may see it and embrace it, and I surrender now any judgment of it." The sounds of Robin's voice offering the prayer opened my heart to Twelve, and I felt hopeful that I would find the healing I was seeking.

Governing Center (GC) coached by Gaia: Twelve, we are going to do a little play now where you are going to be able to come forth and speak up and say what you want to say.

Gaia notices that my twelve-year old has come back into my body but her consciousness is mostly living up in my head.

GC (coached by Gaia): I know you, and I feel you, and I see your pictures. But now our job is to bring all of your essence down into my body because you no longer belong to the Anti-Christ. We are going to show you that. We now invoke the holographic memory of my Twelve, all initiations that were forgotten and denied with the feminine Anti-Christ brides. [Gaia invokes her healing language.] I call back now my will to fight and to live by choice.

Knocking on door signals "Mother" to enter. I go and sit in the chair designated for Twelve.

"Mother": We are coming for you. You are the special one. [There is drumming in background.] We are coming for you, the virgin bride, the bride of the Anti-Christ, the privileged bride. We celebrate you. You are for him. You are the chosen one. You will give yourself over to the Anti-Christ, and we will show you how the woman is the special one. You have the power to claim his power in you. All you have to do is open your legs. Let this animal tickle you.

"Mother" leans back over the chair and opens her legs. She simulates stimulating herself. Twelve looks away from her mother.

"Mother": Oh, the pleasure of the Anti-Christ. You are his bride. The pleasure you will have. Oh, the power. [Mother goes toward Twelve and tries to open her legs which are tightly closed and resisting her efforts.]

"Mother": It is your turn. We are going to show you how to be the bride.

Twelve, standing with and empowered by GC: I do not want
    to be the bride. [My voice is rising in pitch and fury.
    I recoil in horror. My muscles contract in repulsion.]

The practitioner playing my mother chants phrases like 'we
are sacrificing the animal, you are the special one, you get to
do the sacrifice, you have the power'. She tells Twelve that
this is what she has been raised for and that it is a privilege
to be the chosen one. Twelve continues to say she does not
want the power. "Mother" takes Twelve's hand to try and
position her to do the sacrifice.

"Mother": Come Beth, come up to the table and choose.

I, as Twelve, pull back. I feel my strength to resist as my arms
tighten against the side of my body. I do not want to go to the
table. My legs tighten, ready to kick "Mother" as she approaches.

Gaia: Freeze. And (speaking to Twelve) go to the GC chair.
    [She instructs "Mother" to stay where she is.]

GC says to Twelve (coached by Gaia): We get to take off the
    mask. We get to take off the mask. We get to pull
    the masks off and tell mother "no" and tell all the
    women "no". Say, 'the game is over'. So, let us do it
    together (GC and Twelve).

Twelve with GC: [I feel my impulse to fight. Heat rises from
    my stomach moving upwards to my face. There is a
    rush of hot air moving out of my mouth as I deliver
    my words.] No! No! No! No! The game is over.

"Mother": Oh Beth, do not do this.

I am firm and clear in stating my desire. My tense arms are
crossed against my stomach and I hold myself tightly, resisting
Mother's whining.

Twelve with GC: No, I do not want this power.

"Mother": You do not know what you are doing.

Twelve with GC [with determination]: I am taking all of your masks off. I do not want this. I see you.

My hand swiftly moves across their faces, yanking the masks down. Tension and heat explode through my fingertips and wrist. "Mother" is screaming in the background.

Twelve with GC: I see you. I see you.

"Mother": They are going to kill us. They are going to kill us. Stop this, Beth. You are going to be responsible for all this.

I am not influenced by her manipulation. I hold steady in my resolve.

Twelve with GC: I do not want to kill.

"Mother": Let the blood flow, and you will save all of us. You will save all of us. You have the power.

My jaw is set, and my teeth are clenched. Then my mouth opens widely, hoping that my message will pierce the fog of my mother.

Twelve with GC: Mother, wake up. Mother, wake up. Wake up, Mother. They tricked you.

"Mother": Oh Beth.

I am in charge now, and I realize my mother has no power. I see her confusion. A surging river of tingles moves up my legs.

Twelve with GC: We have to get help. We have to get help. Right now.

There is shouting and pandemonium between Twelve and Mother. Twelve is now leading the way as she pushes each leg into the floor, launching herself toward the door. Twelve with GC runs out of the room to get the police. Then they return.

Twelve with GC [My voice is firm and deep]: Everybody! Stop this! You cannot do this. I will not stand for this. This is not me. This is not me. I am not the bride of Satan. I will not kill. I am not the bride of the Anti-Christ.

DISCREATING VOWS, AGREEMENTS TO INVOKE THE ANTI-CHRIST

Gaia coaching, Beth repeats: I now discreate all vows, all agreements, all ritual imprints that I will invoke the rise of Satan or the Anti-Christ. I surrender this agreement from all eternal levels, where they have hooked into my field to do this. NO MORE. NO more.

Gaia invokes sound and healing languages to transmute the energies. With the help of the practitioners in the room, we send all the spirits that were involved in this ritual back to the healing source.

Twelve with GC, addressing the women: You can no longer control me. I am speaking the truth.

I feel a current of strength running through my body as I recreate, for Twelve, that we are safe now, and she is lovable no matter what she has gone through.

GC: I now recreate with you, Twelve, that you are lovable and forgiven.

Gaia supports me to lie down to release my trauma more deeply.

Twelve: I do not want to be a girl. Girls get hurt. I am not safe. I do not want to be a woman. I do not want to feel. I want to die.

GC: I see that your experiences have made you feel unsafe. I understand why you feel that way. [I begin shaking and releasing the fear in my body that being a girl makes me unsafe on this planet. A practitioner has hands on my back. I feel the gripping energies in my spine releasing.]

Gaia guides me to put my hand on my vagina and asks Twelve to come all the way back home and release those decisions.

Gaia: You can get safe once you incarnate all the way. If you come all the way back into your body with forgiveness and self-love, they cannot control you and trick you anymore, for we'll have the wisdom of our body, soul and heart to make choices. [The practitioner helps move the energy down my legs so Twelve can come all the way in.]

We discovered that Twelve was afraid to feel sexual arousal because arousal had been linked to killing. They had aroused her using animals and humans licking her. She was threatened that if she did not kill the rabbit, she would receive a stick up her anus and that they "knew she liked that". So, Twelve was confused because pleasure and pain were linked together. Feeling pleasure moved her into violence, so she shut down stimulation so she would not be violent. My Twelve and I shut down my arousal which has affected my sexuality my whole life.

Twelve had not been able to forgive herself for killing a rabbit. She wanted to die after that. Her decision to shut down had become a form of self-torture in my life because of the loneliness and isolation of not having a partner and my barren landscape in life of not being able to experience feelings or pleasure.

In follow-up work, I allowed my hatred to express through my body, so it did not stay in my tissue creating toxicity. I chose to use a plastic bat and beat pillows, scream, and stomp my feet. As my twelve-year-old alter healed, I was able to forgive my mother's behavior and release the karma of having to punish her in this life or in the future.

After the work with Twelve (this chapter) and Thirty-Two (Chapter Seventeen), we gathered all the alters and all ages, slowly introducing them to one another. Each one only knew itself as an isolated part. They now realized that they were all parts of the same soul stream, and we could then do a multiple integration to link all of them together. For example, I was able to have my thirty-two-year old meet my twelve-year old and my five-year old and my seven-year old and have them all realize that they were part of my soul. Nobody was left out. This is the strategy of weaving myself back to wholeness.

My general understanding now of my psyche and soul is that I could not have had so many alters unless I had been consistently tortured and left my body. I have uncovered memories of violations at many ages that led to splitting. One of the first times I was taught to beat children was discovered during my first Intensive (Chapter Twelve). I had been tortured until I split off, and a part of me was shown how to channel my rage toward another human or animal. I have not described in this book the details and horrors of the babies and animals killed in sacrifice. My main interest is in showing the repair. I now understand the inhuman acts of child abuse and the fracturing and victimization that an individual goes through in order to become a perpetrator. Demonic forces worked through my mother, my sister, me, and anyone who would do ritual abuse. Because it is inhuman, it requires a nonhuman entity to override the human heart. I now understand how someone can be so evil and horrible. They are completely fractured from their core self, and they are trained to be this way. It comes from their unhealed wounds. When I was rageful with Steven, I was playing out the pattern of being violated and channeling my rage toward a child. My seven-year-old child (Chapter Two) split off and "went to the light" while my father and others abused her. These traumas continued throughout my teen years and kept the abuser programming alive in me (Chapter Five). Split off selves of many of my child alters were coupled to create my adult alters.

Through the years of focusing on healing my alters, the healing team and I have come to understand that alters were programmed to come forward by symbols, sounds, smells, signals, sexual arousal, and so forth. (The healing team has used this understanding to help others as well.) An alter was trained to take over the whole psyche and to have complete disassociation from the core. My core self had amnesia about the actions of my alters. The healing foundation that has been laid over time has empowered my present time self with my soul to be strong enough to integrate the memories and experiences of my alters.

My experience has given me an understanding of how my alters were created, how they were trained to kill, and I realize that this is the type of mind control that creates assassins. Some sources say that the CIA has been doing this for years through MK Ultra. Currently there are many individuals suing the government for the MK Ultra mind-control program in the '60s, '70s and '80s (Enos, 2018).

I am now strong enough and able to know that I trained my children in the ways of the cult. The total lack of choice that dominated my training has helped me have compassion for myself and gain understanding of the dynamics of families of ritual abuse. Having a bigger mental picture of how I was abused and how I was mind-controlled to abuse others has expanded my capacity to have compassion for myself; it has also allowed me to share this intellectual understanding through my writing.

Grief sometimes hits me like a tsunami, and all I can do is surrender to this emotion, allowing it to cleanse me. I also experience my heart opening wide with gratitude, expanding in love beyond anything I have known before.

HEALING A PAST LIFE THROUGH FORGIVENESS IN THE PRESENT

After having many, many sessions integrating my alters, I wanted to learn how to forgive my mother and release the karma with my mother and my sons so that I would never need to punish my mother in future lifetimes or receive harm and punishment from my sons as retribution for torturing them. I wanted to be done with these cycles!

The following memory of a past life with my mother and Steven was retrieved in a session. It demonstrates the ongoing relationship of abuse that my mother, my son, and I had played out over many lifetimes with one another. In these sessions, I am cleaning up the cycles of perpetrator/victim/rescuer that we have played out over many lifetimes.

In my intuitive third eye, I see the following. My past life images are validated by intense physical sensations.

I am standing at the edge of a ceremonial fire pit in the presence of the High Priestess, being tested to prove my devotion to the gods we worship. My loyalty must be proven by throwing my brother into the fire pit as a human sacrifice. [As this information emerges, I recoil. There is a knot in the pit of my stomach as I observe the sacrifice unfolding.] *I am told it is a great honor to be sacrificed to the gods. I do not really want to do this because I love my brother deeply. But I must deny my personal will and prove that I am willing to comply with the demands of my community. I do not dare anger the gods by refusing this sacrifice. This could bring dire consequences to my people if I go against our rituals. I throw him into the pit to his death, his screams filling my ears as his flesh meets the fire.*

My heavy heart is sinking into my chest, contracting in sorrow, as I view the events. In present time, I am aware that my heart contracts with the knowing of shutting my heart down in that Mayan moment, and that has bled through to my current relationship with Steven. I am shrouded in guilt. As I experience this knowing about my mother's and my son's souls, my whole body is wracked with grief. I feel the truth of who these souls are. The soul that I am sacrificing in this Mayan lifetime is Steven, and the High Priestess is now my mother.

We set two chairs facing one another. My Governing Center will talk with my Priestess from the Mayan life. She tells me her name is Akna.

Governing Center (GC): I invoke the part of my soul that was a Mayan Priestess named Akna.

Switch chairs.

My skin feels cool and tingles as I acknowledge Akna and her presence in my body. I feel a heavy blanket of shame sitting on my shoulders.

GC: Do you know you are a part of my Soul?

Switch chairs.

Akna: No, I do not know about you.

GC: I am a future lifetime of your soul. I, Beth, am now healing the energies of many of my lifetimes, including yours. What happened to you in your lifetime that left you with guilt?

Akna: I had to do what the High Priestess asked of me. I had to sacrifice my brother and go against my own love and knowing.

GC: So, you did not feel you could go against the High Priestess even though it went against something inside of you?

Akna: I was not allowed to have my own feelings, much less show them. Our religion and gods requiring sacrifice were the only thing that mattered. I was devastated when I was required to sacrifice my own brother, but I could not show that. Nothing else could prove my loyalty because they knew I loved him. Males were considered less important than females.

Gaia: There is a parallel between that lifetime and your current life, Beth. You have continued participating in rituals with your mother in this lifetime. Are you ready to break the energetic contract with your mother?

I feel deep waves of sorrow moving from my solar plexus up through my heart, and my rage follows. I move onto a mat so that I can kick and scream, expressing and freeing up these energies that course through my body. With each kick and punch, I feel the restricting energies leaving my body. It is time for me to reclaim my freedom to follow my own love.

Gaia: Our bodies are sacred; hurting another is never in divine alignment.

Our session ended, and I continued to integrate forgiveness which opened my heart to self-love. After all sessions that were based in trauma memory where I hurt others, we would send blessings and prayers and ask for forgiveness with the souls that participated with me. This would release myself and them from being tied to one another, no longer karmically bound. In every session of uncovering trauma and rituals, the practitioners helped me do this cleansing process of reconciliation.

CLAIMING COCREATION: A PATH TO FORGIVENESS AND FREEING MY SOUL

Understanding the lifetime I had with my mother and my son showed me how my soul continued to incarnate with their souls to try to heal the relationships. Based on the energy frequency of unhealed self-hatred and condemnation from sacrificing my Mayan brother, I was then attracted in this lifetime into a family where I would experience perpetration. **I have discovered through soul dialog that desire for revenge magnetically binds souls together.** For me, doing the soul work allowed me to end the karma and to sustain forgiveness between our souls and end the revenge matrix. I realized later in life as my children grew older, that my horrific guilt caused me to want to rescue them. Rescuing them does not complete the karma. If I feel responsible for another soul, they then feel controlled and end up victimizing me to try and get free, and we are in the cycle once again. Each soul is responsible and cocreates the victim/victimizer/rescuer dance. This is not an excuse to be a victimizer, but it lends more compassion and understanding of why we would ever incarnate and continue to repeat these patterns. It helps illustrate how and why the cycle of abuse continues.

I see now that the roles are often swapped amongst the players from one lifetime to the next. If I do not forgive myself and my mother at this time, but only desire revenge for her role in my torture in this life, then I will return to play this out in another life and nothing is healed. I could not have healed this without my soul's willingness to take responsibility for its cocreation.

Rescuer dynamics inside of me also links me back to the codependent matrix where my actions are motivated by guilt. When guilt arises from our actions as a victimizer, and we try to fix another out of guilt, we become a rescuer. The rescuer role is fueled by guilt, forgetting we are co-creators. However, when each soul remembers that all the players involved are cocreating experiences together, there is no need for guilt. In fact, guilt carried by a victimizer distracts the victim from taking responsibility for his or her own creation. As I held guilt for what I did to my sons, it allowed them to treat me terribly. I attracted harm from other people. Guilt pulls in more harm because I do not feel that I deserve to be treated well. My sons would act out on me, and I did not have the strength to set a boundary for their behavior. Through self-love and forgiveness, I empowered my ability to set boundaries around cruel behavior.

I have deep remorse for the harm that I brought to my children. My remorse has allowed me to know that I never want to create harm with another again. Some of my greatest pain is that I have not been able to fully heal with both of my sons. Steven has gotten healthier with healing work; Nicholas has struggled with mental health issues and has sought advice only from a psychiatrist who prescribes drugs. Our society does not support the idea of cocreation and does not understand that in addition to actions, it is beliefs, frequency, consciousness, and vibration that creates physical reality. Without this journey, *I* would not have understood that as well. Cocreation and understanding how consciousness fits together among people and families gives me the power to heal my side of the cocreation which then frees me and is an invitation for another to get free, but they don't always choose to do so. I have no control of whether my sons heal or not.

CHAPTER NINETEEN

Liberating My Soul and Body from the Satanic Matrix

HOW GUILT AND SHAME IS PART OF THE SATANIC MATRIX

I know the timbre, taste, texture, smell, frequency, sensations, and suppression of shame and guilt. The Healing Team and I have discovered that guilt and shame are not true emotions. **Guilt and shame come from a frequency matrix intended to control and suppress emotional healing. They serve the Satanic Matrix.** Robin says to me, "Guilt and shame are matrices of energy that continue to suppress memory and feeling worthy of love so that we can't repair. They are often infused through religious and spiritual manipulation. We see this in priest abuse of children. The shame is passed, energetically, from the abuser to the children, holding the vow of secrecy. The energy and often entities are passed from perpetrator to child. Pedophilia, in its very nature, is generated from unhealed children victims, moving into adulthood, and perpetuating the cycle of abuse."

Robin tells me, "If you continue to blame yourself and beat yourself up, you will never heal. Shame has a neurological frequency that shuts down the brain to keep you from feeling and remembering in your body. It is anchored in unworthiness, and in order to heal, you must claim your worth as a human being and eternal soul."

"Yes, I have experienced how shame and guilt completely thwart my ability to uncover my own truth," I replied. "I experience shame like a heavy, wet blanket enveloping me. There is no flow or memories that can move into my awareness when I am in shame, and I feel totally unworthy."

Robin has shared, as she works with her clients, me, and herself, that it requires every dimension of healing to get shame to move: body, soul, emotion, and mind. "In order to lift shame, one has to choose to feel the emotional body. Emotional catharsis starts to defrost the controls that shame holds. There are entities and possessions holding shame in place. Psychological counseling can bring compassion and understanding, but it takes energy work, spiritual power, to transmute the matrix of shame. The ancestors carry shame as well. Self-love, forgiveness in the soul and body, the love from Source, and the love from other are all needed to transmute shame." I had to move through shame and guilt so I could integrate my alters and heal my soul.

I now appreciate my choice to face the abuse I passed to my children. Once I made it conscious, I could start to move, heal, and forgive, as painful as it was. Shame and guilt drives depression, mental illness and suicide which are often symptoms of anyone who has experienced incest, pedophilia, and ritual abuse. I faced the circumstances and aspects of me that had led to the abuse, I discovered my false perceptions, and I moved the energies out of my body. I brought forth my loving intentions and created new imprints that supported repair, forgiveness, and compassion.

FORGIVENESS, SELF-LOVE, AND REUNITING WITH SOURCE

Some say that if we are co-creating with another and we have both chosen the experience, there is nothing to forgive. From an intellectual stance, that is true. But I see forgiveness as an emotional experience that reflects a state of being which can lead me back to peace within my heart. True forgiveness comes from my heart, not my mind. It is the release and transformation of specific emotions that signal forgiveness to me. And on that basis, I deeply desire forgiveness for my own sense of well-being. By loving my shadow, it no longer runs me.

The healing journey is not solely a matter of gaining information about what happened, because knowledge alone does not heal. Love is the healing power that can be supported by knowledge. Robin once said to me, "Beth, having all the information about what happened is not going to free you. Having the essence of love in your body radiating every moment, that's going to feel like freedom."

Ultimately, the place where I have most keenly felt separation is where I did not feel lovable by God. I judged myself harshly and thought that my shadow was so dark that I was eternally damned and damaged, deserving to be cast out. Realizing that I am part of Source that descended into form and journeyed on behalf of the expansion of Source, I feel my worthiness to return to the love from whence I came. The wisdom of my journey, gained by not staying in the bliss and the light, has allowed me to remember that I am all of it, and I am worthy of love. My journey has created the indelible imprint in my soul that I am part of Source returning to love and returning to my original innocence after a long, long journey of separation.

My idea of God as a deity has evolved into God, Source, as a dynamic expression in infinite forms including us earthlings and our experiences. Source is experiencing itself through me, as well as the stars, the earth, the space in between, earthlings, other beings, animals, plant life, and All That Is.

As I reflect upon my life, if I look through the lens of duality, I see myself as a victim, a violated human. There is good, there is evil. Through this lens, perpetrators are evil humans who must be punished. As the feeling of being victimized rises, I wonder what punishment is due for these crimes. But I have learned that punishment does not bring healing, and most often it perpetuates the violence that it is meant to deter. I know that perpetrators were once victims, so there is no such thing as someone who is only a perpetrator. So, when I feel helpless, wanting to annihilate all the evildoers that are hurting innocent children, I go within to find my own perpetrator and my hurting child victim that led to creating a perpetrator in me, and I bring compassion and love to both aspects of myself. They are both parts of me.

As practitioners, Robin, Joseph and Ahara have also had to look at their perpetrator, victim, and rescuer aspects on a soul level in order to personally evolve and help me. We have all realized that our spiritual purpose is to bring deep compassion and healing for humans. We have sought to come out of separation for our individual growth as well as in service to humanity. It has been a full community commitment to learn how to heal these horrific experiences that have been perpetuated for eons of time, that we believe are the cause of war and violence on this earth.

LIVING IN THE PRESENT FROM MY HEART WITH COMPASSION

It is 2020. I am soaking in a hot springs pool, looking at the watermelon colored rocks that sweep up toward the sky. I hear the caw of the crows and see the shadow of their wings float by on the water. The heat and moisture reach deep into my muscles, soothing my soul, and my nostrils widen as I breathe in crisp air, filling my lungs with joy. *I am living the good life. I am so grateful for this beauty. It is inside of me too.*

I come out of the springs, watching the drops land beneath me. I check my phone and see a text. "Oh, it's Nicholas." I sigh with a bit of relief. "Hey Mom, just checking in. How are you doing today?" I am so glad to hear from him. I miss him.

"Doing well. I just finished a soak and a four-and-a-half-mile walk. How are you doing?" My heart swells with gratitude, and I sigh.

The next morning, I get a phone call from Sarah, a young woman in my healing community. She is struggling with grounding a job and a place to live. "Hi Beth. Are you going to African dance class this morning?"

"Yes," I reply. "I love that class."

"I want to go but I don't think I am safe to drive myself right now. I feel like I am out of my body, and I am spinning." Sarah's voice has a pitch of desperation, much higher than usual.

I pick her up, and as she gets into my car, I look into her eyes. I observe that she is in a trauma memory in a disassociated state, something that I know well. "I keep experiencing time as speeding up and slowing down. My thoughts are jumping around. It's very, very strange," she says.

Tears of compassion well up as I recognize myself in her. I reach out and touch her hand. "Just keep breathing deeply and focusing on your breath," I say. "It's going to be okay."

I am at a Potluck dinner organized by my community. I look around and notice many guests, some of whom I recognize, but there are many new faces, as well. "Hello. It's so nice to have you with us." I smile. I feel a buzz of excitement in my stomach, aware that I will soon be sharing with this group of thirty-five curious souls about my healing journey. After we eat, we gather in a circle. As I look around, a deep silence envelops the room, and soon it is my turn. I begin to speak. "Growing up I never knew there was any such thing as a heart's desire. I used to live a split life, numb, depressed, and disconnected. During the day I was a good little girl following the rules of my home and church. At night, I was taken to rituals and participated in cult activities. My story is one of facing my deepest shadow and choosing love."

I continue to share with the group. Then I conclude, "My heart's desire has become my passion for healing myself." As I speak, my voice is clear and steady. I look around the room and see compassion in the eyes of many. I am grateful for the open hearts who are willing to receive my story. I feel my own heart expand as I speak my truth. My body is relaxed, a pleasant warmth envelops me. There was a time where the threat of death silenced me. Now, I am free to tell my truth.

"You are so courageous, Beth," several of my closest supporters say.

"This is what I am meant to do. This is what gives my life purpose," I reply. I look at their shining faces. Tears roll down my cheeks. My suffering has purpose which is to help and inspire others.

MY PRAYER FOR THOSE WHO KEEP THE SECRETS

Through writing this book, I have integrated and healed on a deeper, cellular level, than from the original sessions that I have described. My secrets are no more. I feel liberated when my life's story can help others awaken and heal. My purpose is not only to expose the underbelly of separation trauma and denials that control so many of us but to inspire courage, healing, and freedom. That is the gift I receive by sharing my story. We can all liberate ourselves with courage, commitment, love, and forgiveness. I am beyond grateful for the opportunity to be part of the liberation that is now at hand. This is what makes my life make sense. It is my legacy.

Curiosity about life and what the future holds has replaced dread. I am no longer looking over my shoulder wondering where the next attack is coming from. My life is hardly perfect, but it is now flowing. Currently I am participating in a community that is committed to healing their shadow and not reenacting their pain onto each other. I am held by people who are choosing love. I am safe because we are committed to conscious, loving communication with each other.

Where I have encountered evil, I have had to bring love, for evil is anchored in false beliefs about myself and the source of love. The beliefs of separation are that I am powerless unless I dominate, I am worthless unless I control, and I am 'less than' so I must impose authority over others. Essentially, I am separate from love, so I must take.

Evil is what occurs in human behavior when we feel separate from, i.e. lacking, love. I have noticed that the word *evil* is the word *live* spelled backwards. Evil is the twisting of the life sustaining force, the result of believing lies about who we are, the belief that love is outside of ourselves. Evil seeks to thwart the flow of love. To fully live is to embrace all parts of ourselves, including the twisted "evil" parts, and to repair their beliefs, compassionately bringing love to what we have labeled unlovable. My greatest healing happens through loving presence of the moment.

In my healing journey, there have been so many moments where I could barely see what my next step was, but as I lifted my foot with the intent of moving forward and choosing life, a ground of support formed beneath me. There has always been a divine spirit protecting me, cheering me on, whispering in my ear that I *was* lovable, remaining present with me, standing as a sentinel to my awakening and remembering the innocent being that I truly am.

My greatest desire is that all who read this book can receive blessings and encouragement for their own journey. Return to your own heart and reclaim your worth and innocence. You deserve love, no matter what!

Epilogue

The principles of Soul Alchemy™ that were grounded over the years of doing my healing work have birthed a community of people that are evolving soul/body unity. The Center for Sustainable Love is now training practitioners using Rainbow Light practices and Soul Alchemy™ trainings that I utilize in sustaining my health and wellness. Having lived in relationships and groups for so many years that were torturous, finding a community that offers love and kindness has allowed a rebirth for me. This community is a resource for me to sustain love and growth.

There are many individuals who are awakening to the need for a new way of living on this planet. Most communities that intend to create a life with shared resources fail because the shadow energies do not get addressed, and the separation energies quickly divide those who originally wanted to live in harmony. With a group who are committed to healing the separation and doing their shadow work consistently and diligently, it is now possible for unity in community to be sustained.

Those who are drawn to The Center for Sustainable Love and desire to practice the principles of Soul Alchemy™ are in the process of healing their own issues. We have found that it no longer takes fifteen years to heal! Those who want to heal ritual abuse can now heal more quickly because a foundation has been laid through the years of healing work that Dawn and I and others have done. We have been the point of the arrow blazing an energetic healing path for others. Much of the healing now happens in groups because the power of the group energy is so dynamic. Also, the energies of evolution that now are upon this planet are greatly assisting the process, and it is much quicker than our journey was. The old structures are crumbling and the opportunity to build a loving, compassionate way of living and being is calling to us all right now!

Glossary

Alter – Alters are often considered the multiple personality states being present in one with dissociative identity disorder (DID DSM-5 criteria). These personality states must each have their own enduring pattern of perceiving, relating to and thinking about the environment and self. Alters involve marked discontinuity in sense of self and sense of agency, accompanied by related changes in affect, behavior, consciousness, memory, perception, cognition, and/or sensory-motor functioning. From: www.healthyplace.com/abuse/dissociative-identity-disorder/dissociative-identity-disorder-did-dsm-5-criteria

According to Robin/Gaia: What you call alters are personality structures that have different behaviors that are triggered by certain stimuli that are in the body. Often the alters are in another dimension and are fractured in different aspects of the unconscious and the soul.

Anti-Christ – Anti-Christ is a term used in the satanic ritual community as a force that divides, separates, and holds itself above all other humans. It is also a being that has been projected upon as the antithesis of healing and love for humanity, guided by Satan. Many believe that the Anti-Christ is a physical being that will show up in a body.

Ascended Masters – The commonly known Ascended Masters that are channeled frequently are our human spiritual elder brothers and sisters who have gone beyond the reincarnational wheel of our 3D Earth. They have not achieved true ascended mastery which would take them outside of our dimensional system or time matrix. Many humans that think they are channeling masters are channeling astral entities who are misrepresenting themselves. An Ascended Master is a highly evolved group level of consciousness that exists beyond the dimensions of the Time matrix. They are not in a form as we would know it. (Lisa Renee at https://ascensionglossary.com/index.php/Ascended_Master)

Breathwork – A psycho/spiritual/therapeutic activity that involves the conscious alteration of natural breathing patterns for the purposes of awakening new levels of awareness through activating altered states of consciousness. Breathwork is used to bypass the rational mind and get deeply into cellular memory as well as soul memory. Holotropic breath work is a technique often used by psychiatrists. There are many forms of breathwork.

Chair Polarity Dialog – The original chair work is from Gestalt therapy. John Chitty further developed this work by creating Chair Polarity Dialog. This process divides awareness into two polarities so an individual can clarify various aspects of self such as their inner children, soul parts, or understanding who is making subconscious decisions in their life.

Christ consciousness – Christ consciousness is not connected to any religious modality. It is a frequency created in every human heart once someone chooses the unified field of unconditional love, self-forgiveness, and forgiveness of others.

Co-Creator – Co-Creator describes the principle of having vibrational, matching energies between two people, such that we attract aspects of our self to our self, in relationships and experiences. Thus, all events are cocreated from eternal soul, but not always consciously chosen by the personality. Co-Creation also can refer to a collaborative field of conscious creation among people.

Creator – Creator is a term often used to refer to our source of existence. It is also used to describe an embodiment of our source working through us and is a proclamation that we all are one with our creator by being creators on the earth. It includes the understanding that all of us have the creative power of Source and are always creating all the time in the physical world from our souls, our choices, and our personality.

Deprogramming – Deprogramming is the process of releasing someone from brainwashing, typically that of a religious cult, by the systematic re-imprinting of human love and safety.

Discreation/Re-creation Process – Discreation/Re-creation is a Soul Alchemy™ healing process. Discreation is the term used for the process of releasing the energetic structures of all limitations, vows, curses, and beliefs that have suppressed the authentic nature of an individual's freewill to love themselves and reclaim wholeness. It involves invoking the will of love to dismantle with movement, sound, breath, and proclamation through the voice. Recreation aligns the multidimensional self with the belief systems and vibrations that align with health, self-love, loving relationships, fulfillment of dreams, creating empowerment consciousness that supports the reality of any individual's heart desires. This is done through movement sound, proclamation, voice, and accessing the will of love in the multidimensional reality of soul/body unity.

DNA – Deoxyribonucleic acid is a molecule that carries the genetic instructions used in the growth, development, functioning, and reproduction of living organisms. In Soul Alchemy™ work, we access the vibration of DNA, the consciousness that has been inherited from relatives and ancestors, and we can re-engage DNA characteristics through positive life force love energy, thereby activating DNA characteristics that have been dormant for the purpose of healing and evolution.

Dimensions – A dimension is a state of consciousness and a means of organizing different planes of existence according to the vibratory rate of that which exists. Each dimension has certain sets of laws and principles that are specific to the frequency of that dimension. The most commonly acknowledged dimension on this earth is the third dimension where one exists in a physical body. From: www.illuminology. tumblr.com/post/55526706444/the-12-dimensions-explained

The soul retrieval process integrates all dimensions of soul into a harmonious balance of all soul parts. In Soul Alchemy™, Rainbow Light is used for multidimensional soul integration.

Dissociation – Moving one's consciousness out of the body so that one is not aware of what is happening in the body, which creates lack of continuity between thoughts, memories, surroundings, actions, and identity. The psychiatric definition refers to being split off (a component of mental activity) to act as an independent part. In Soul Alchemy™, dissociation also acknowledges the fractured soul parts that have left the physical plane and carry emotional content and experiences of other lives.

Divinity – Divinity is a concept referring to coming from Source, a god, supreme being, creator or spirits. In Soul Alchemy™, all is divine, even the shadow.

Entity – An entity is a discarnate or non-physical being that attaches itself to a person, energy field, or soul part, to serve the unconscious or conscious desire of a person. Through this attachment the entity affects the physical, emotional, and/or mental health of the host; the entity can cause problems or aggravate existing ones; it can also lead the host to criminal behavior and addictions. In Soul Alchemy™, entities are always in service to the client, even if they are demonic, and they can be removed with love.

Epigenetics – Epigenetics is the study of how certain genes are read by the cells and can be transformed based on a social, physical milieu, and activation through frequency, new behavior, new environments, meditations, and activities, which have been proven to change the DNA expression of a human being.

Gaia – Gaia is a term often used to refer to the spiritual consciousness of earth. However, Gaia is also the name of a part of Robin that can see the eternal soul through all dimensions and looks for the cause in our consciousness for what is happening in current time. These two uses of the term Gaia are not synonymous, but they are connected. Robin's Gaia is in service to healing all wounds on earth.

Galactic Beings – A term used to refer to soul parts and physical beings who are not from earth and have identified with other planetary origins, such as Venus, the Pleiades, or Sirius, for example.

Governing Center – The Governing Center is the guiding source of wholeness for each person that allows for unity among body and soul. This is the conscious, current self that resides in the heart and takes into consideration the wants and needs of all aspects of self.

Holographic Reality – Holographic fields are the composite of all that we are, expressing through our fields in the world. Our holographic realities attract to us energies that match what we are pulsing out into the world. In Soul Alchemy™, the holographic field of an individual is our vibrational field in present time that is impacted by both conscious and unconscious, known and unknown, experiences. It is like a one-thousand-piece jigsaw puzzle that is multidimensional, impacted by the genetics of our ancestors, our belief systems in current time, our choices, our strengths, our weaknesses, our actions, our disease patterns. It is the field where all of our being is vibrating a story.

"I AM" Activity – A movement founded in the 1930s by Guy and Edna Ballard whose teachings centered on Ascended Masters. It was a forerunner to New Age philosophy. In my experience, this church coupled with satanic rituals.

Implants – Microorganism and/or energy devices that can be physical or nonphysical that serve to control or direct human behavior. They affect the overall well-being, and limit sovereignty and conscious cocreation of the desires we wish. They are often created through abductions, rituals, intentional CIA/MK Ultra experimentation and can be removed.

Imprint – The frequency signature of an experience that moves into the tissue, the holographic field, and eventually the subconscious. It becomes a deep, unconscious reality, for example, "life is unsafe".

Inner Child – The consciousness of our child experiences that is often held in our subconscious body memory. The inner child has a vibration, a belief, a consciousness, and a form. Sometimes the inner child is integrated into health through repair; sometimes it is vibrating the damage of past traumas.

Intensive – A retreat of several days during which a client, based on specific intentions, undergoes a variety of healing modalities which address the needs of the soul.

MK Ultra – A government program employing mind-control to train individuals to be useful for its desired social, political, and cultural agendas by splitting participants' minds through torture and training, resulting in complete compartmentalization, unaware activity, split personalities, and complete manipulation of the conscious self.

Rainbow Light Energy Tool – An energetic practice developed by Robin Duda and Ahara Vatter to facilitate direct connection with the Source of one's being. All aspects of one's Soul can be accessed through this practice. The purpose of the Rainbow Light Energy Tool is to empower our will and our soul with unity consciousness to amplify our resources for the embodiment of love. It facilitates the activation of conscious soul retrieval, clearing our energy field, and centering ourselves to establish Governing Center, which is the guiding force in all the healing work.

Satanic Matrix – The satanic matrix is a visceral, energetic, holographic field that vibrates the intentions of entities and manipulation forces with the intention of domination, control, invoking terror and fear in humans. It is a field that consumes, holds, and separates soul and astral energy away from an individual's wholeness.

Satanic Ritual Abuse (SRA) – Satanic Ritual Abuse is an extreme, sadistic form of abuse of children and nonconsenting adults. It is methodic, systematic sexual, physical, emotional, and spiritual abuse, which often includes mind control, torture, and highly illegal and immoral activities such as murder, child pornography, and prostitution. (Wikipedia)

Shadow – The unknown or unseen aspects of self that have not been expressed or acknowledged and may be disowned as part of self due to being judged as flaws or even perceived as evil aspects.

Somatic – Relating to the sensations in the body that are governed by the nervous system and are observable by the mind. They are experienced as non-left-brain, logical experiences such as tingling in my arms, tightness in the belly, wobbly knees, and so forth.

Soul – The vibrational container of the sum of one's experiences as a being who has participated in all realms and dimensions and is ever-evolving and expanding. The Soul also has identity, desires, needs, wants, dreams, contracts, and multiple forms. The Soul is multidimensional and is mostly experienced through somatics, emotions, and sensations.

Soul Alchemy™ – Soul Alchemy™ is a spiritual, healing practice developed through the Sustainable Love healing team and was specifically grounded by Joseph and Robin Duda, and Ahara Vatter. Soul Alchemy™ is a multidimensional, conscious evolutionary process that creates healing through one's soul, body, and heart partnership. Through this partnership, there is an alchemy that allows for our human personal freedom, joy, internal and external unity. It is a process of choosing wholeness, compassion, and self-love. It is a spiritual philosophy of living that honors all life and each individual's right to their own soul's path. Wholeness is empowered through the equal value between spirit and body. Soul Alchemy™ is grounded in the wisdom that our soul's embodiment is for the purpose of growth and spiritual learning. (See Appendix)

Soul Retrieval – The process of bringing back energies of the Soul that have been fragmented or disassociated into the tissue for conscious love, bonding, and integration.

Sovereignty – The energetic, physical, and emotional experience of being free; full right and power over oneself without interference from outside sources.

Appendix

THE PRINCIPLES OF SOUL ALCHEMY™

1. We are eternal beings with many forms, all a part of our source. Our soul is multi-dimensional. This life is a gift that our souls have chosen, and our journey as humans can be conscious or not. Soul Alchemy™ is a partnership of conscious soul evolution.

2. While in this incarnation, our spirit and body are one. We have a choice to experience wholeness. The soul-spirit self is learning through and from the physical creations, and the body personal self is learning from the soul-spirit. Our awakening then creates an opportunity to consciously unify any fragments of soul into wholeness through our body and free will. This is called conscious soul evolution.

3. Our inner and outer realities are one. Our consciousness is always being demonstrated and reflected on the outside. The inner landscape or hologram is created from vibration

and electro-magnetic fields generated by multidimensional beliefs, vows, identities, decisions, DNA, ancestral imprints, spiritual attachments and inner relational dynamics among the soul parts and the personality. These inner states impact all the bodies, astral-emotional, mental, etheric, and physical. And all these realms impact our inner consciousness.

4. Empowerment comes from our personal responsibilities and free will choice to become a conscious co-creator with the universe and others. If we want to see a change in our reality, we must stay in the commitment to inner unity and love and choose the behaviors and relationships that serve nourishment and expansion of our authentic nature and others. We then choose to transform separation into love and freedom. We bring unconsciousness to consciousness. Transformation involves inside work and outer behavioral change.

5. All human beings have a right to personal empowerment and evolution no matter what their karma or past experiences. Each individual has a right to their inner healer, eternal soul, and alchemist. We have a right to our needs, feelings, and wants and to live life in happiness and to pursue our greatest joy and soul's purpose. We have a right to experience freedom, safety, and love on this earth plane. This is the power of the Governing Center to hold this knowing for the self.

6. As conscious co-creators, we choose to evolve the soul and heal the separation. The process of the soul's evolution calls forward the integration and resolution of the soul as victim, victimizer, and rescuer. If these aspects are denied and/or prominent, it creates separation. We then have journeys of blame, negativity, abuse, dominance, power over and under dynamics. These aspects are seeking to heal in the spiritual, emotional, physical, mental realms, and we then

discover more self-love, self-forgiveness, free choice, and empowerment in our lives.

7. Love is the healer, the mega juice and unifier of all.

Reprinted with permission from: Robin and Joseph Duda, Co-Founders, Sustainable Love Training & Guidance Center

Annotated Resources

Chitty, J. (2017, March 2). *Explaining the Polarity Therapy Two Chair Method* [Video file]. Retrieved from https://www.bing.com/videos/search?q=youtube+john+chitty&view=detail&mid=6D2038A5B4D1854C76EB6D2038A5B4D1854C76EB&FORM=VIRE

Chitty, J. (2017, March 2). *Origins of Polarity Therapy* [Video file]. Retrieved from https://www.bing.com/videos/search?q=John+Chitty+polarity+therapy+youtube&docid=608030767185397494&mid=EB4DFCCC098025714CA6EB4DFCCC098025714CA6&view=detail&FORM=VIRE

Recommended for those who want to understand Polarity Therapy whose principles are used in chair dialog work in Soul Alchemy ™. Chitty discusses Dr. Randolph Stone and the many influences on Stone's development of Polarity Therapy.

Enos, R. (2018, May 25). Survivors from the MK Ultra Program Come Together To Sue the Federal Government. Retrieved from https://www.collective-evolution.com/2018/05/25/survivors-from-the-mk-ultra-program-come-together-with-plans-to-sue-the-federal-government/

Gestalt Therapy (Simply Explained). (2017, October 15). Retrieved from https://www.youtube.com/watch?v=GBl14hIqDwc

This is a quick overview of the principles of Gestalt Therapy developed by Fritz Perls.

Icke, D. (1998). *The Biggest Secret.* Amazon.

This author has written many books about the hidden and not-so-hidden forces influencing life on our planet. He was one of the first authors who validated the atrocities I was discovering in the '90s and discussed the agenda by the elite of controlling the masses and enslaving humanity.

Illuminology. *The 12 dimensions explained.* www.illuminology. tumblr.com/post/55526706444/the-12-dimensions-explained

There are many different ideas about the dimensions. If you are curious about them, this would be one site to explore.

O'Brien, C. (1995). *Trance Formation of America.* Amazon.

O'Brien, C. (2004). *Access Denied: For Reasons of National Security.* Amazon.

O'Brien's books reveal how mind-control programming pervades the highest levels of authority in the United States of America. This book is highly recommended for those who wish to know more about the forces influencing the United States of America.

Oksana, C. (1994). *Safe Passage to Healing.* New York: HarperCollins.

This book is a very compassionate collection of memories and recovery stories of many who experienced satanic ritual abuse. This was the very first book I read once I began to connect with trauma memories.

Renee, L. (2017). Sananda. Lisa Renee Report, November 11th, 2017. Retrieved from https://sananda.website/lisa-renee-report-november-11th-2017/

This article provides understanding about the false light and impostor beings who have manipulated and deceived us humans. This describes the essence of the satanic or Luciferian deception that has impacted everyone on earth. She also sheds light on the concept of an Ascended Master.

Sams, J. and Carson, D. (1999). *Medicine Cards*. New York: St. Martin's Press.

These cards reveal the medicine available to us from the animal kingdom.

Svali. (2019). DeprogramWiki. *Addressing Common Challenges to Healing Work – Svali Blog Post 2019*. Retrieved from https://deprogramwiki.com/svali/svali-blog-posts/addressing-common-challenges-to-healing-work-svali-blog-post-2019/

This article reveals the complex nature of mind-control programming and how programs are installed to prevent the experiencer from remembering. Her extensive knowledge and understanding of SRA and mind-control programming makes a huge contribution toward educating those interested in this topic.

Tracy, N. (2015). HealthyPlace. *Dissociative Identity Disorder (DID) DSM-5 Criteria*. Retrieved from https://www.healthyplace.

com/abuse/dissociative-identity-disorder/dissociative-identity-disorder-did-dsm-5-criteria

This site offers traditional psychological definitions of terms related to dissociative identity disorder (formerly known as multiple personalities) according to the Diagnostic and Statistical Manual, 5th edition, published by the American Psychological Association.